Math Terms and Defi

By Mark J. Curry

Copyright © 2012

Mark J. Curry

All rights reserved. No part of this book may be reproduced in any form without permission, in writing, from the author/publisher.

Introduction

Have you ever wondered what a particular math term means? Are you doing math research? How about a math writing assignment or writing a research paper regarding a mathematical concept or topic? One usually thinks of math in relation to numbers, but math is much more than that. In order to be able to work the numbers and solve the problems an individual needs to know mathematical terms and their meanings. This eBook will help unravel the vocabulary you need to know to be successful with your mathematical journey. From basic arithmetic, to pre-algebra, geometry, ratio and proportions, algebra, measurements and graphs, statistics, and some trigonometry, this learning tool provides more than 800 mathematical terms and their definitions. Enjoy!

Table of Contents

A – Abacus through Axis of Symmetry
B – Balance through Breadth
C – Calandar through Cylinder
D – Data through Dozen
E – Eccentricity through Exterior Angle
F – Face through Fundamental Theorem of Arithmetic
G – Gallon through Grouping
H – Half through Hypotenuse
I – Icosahedron through Iterative
J – Jump Strategy
K – Kilo through Km/h
L – Lateral Surface Area through Lowest Terms
M – MAB Blocks through Mutually Exclusive Events
N – Natural Number through Numerator
O – Oblique through Oval
P – Pair through Pythagorean Theorem
Q – Quadrangle through Quotient
R – Radian through Run
S – S.I. Units through Symmetry
T – Table through Two-dimensional
U – Undecagon through US Standard Units
V – Value through Vulgar Fraction
W – Week through World Time Zones
X – X-axis through X-intercept
Y – Yard through Y-intercept
Z – Zero through Zero (of a function)
Final Thoughts
About the Author

A – Abacus through Axis of Symmetry

Abacus – An abacus is a manual computing device, or calculating tool, that has movable counters. These counters slide on parallel rods and are attached to a frame.

Abscissa – Abscissa is the distance along the horizontal axis, the x-coordinate, on the coordinate plane. The y-coordinate is called the ordinate.

Absolute Value – When referring to real numbers, the absolute value is the numerical value of a number. Absolute value ignores any signs. The absolute value of 8 is 8. The absolute value of -8 is 8. A good rule to remember is that the absolute value is the distance of a number from zero on a number line.

Abundant Number – A number such that the sum of all its divisors (factors), not including itself, is greater than the number itself. Example: Twelve (12) is an abundant number. The factors of 12, not including itself, are 1, 2, 3, 4, and 6. This equals 16, which is greater than 12. Twenty-eight (28) is not an abundant number. The factors of 28, not including itself, are 1, 2, 4, 7, and 14. This equals 28, which is not greater than 28. The first ten abundant numbers are 12, 18, 20, 24, 30, 36, 40, 42, 48, and 54 (also see deficient numbers)

Acre (ac.) – an acre, which is a unit of area, is usually associated with the measurement of land. It equals 43,560 square feet. A square mile consists of 640 acres.

Acute Angle – A geometry term, an acute angle is the measure of an angle that is greater than 0° but less than 90° (° = degrees). If the measure of an angle is greater than 90 degrees, the angle is obtuse.

Acute Triangle – In a triangle, all three interior angles must be less than 90 degrees. Therefore, the triangle is an acute triangle. If any of the interior angles is 90 degrees or more, it is no longer an acute triangle. A triangle that has an interior angle of 90 degrees it is called a right triangle. A triangle that has an interior angle greater than 90 degrees it is called an obtuse triangle.

Add – To combine, or increase, two or more numbers using the operation of addition.

Addend – Any and all numbers that are added together. 3 + 7 + 8 = 18. The 3, 7, and 8 are all addends. The 18 is called the sum.

Addition – The operation in math that adds, finds, or totals the combining of two or more numbers. Addition is also referred to as finding the sum of two or more numbers.

Additive Identity – The most familiar is the set, using the operation of addition, where the additive identity uses the number zero. Example: 7 + 0 = 7 = 0 + 7

Additive Inverse – The additive inverse of a number is the number's negative. The sum of the pair of numbers will equal zero. The additive inverse of 8 is -8. Adding these two numbers together equals zero.

Adjacent Angles – Adjacent angles are "next" to each other. An adjacent angle is two angles that have a common side and a common vertex (This is the point where the angles meet).

Algebra – Letters are substituted for numbers, and the numbers are the constants. An algebraic equation is one where an operation is performed on one side of the equals sign, and the same operation is performed on the other side of the equals sign, sort of like balancing out a scale. The numbers are manipulated in various forms, based on the rules of algebra, to represent sets of values, numbers, vectors, and so forth.

Algebraic Numbers – Numbers that are solutions to polynomial equations. These polynomials have rational coefficients, and include all integers, rational, and some irrational numbers. An algebraic number is a root of a polynomial equation.

Algorithm – An algorithm is a step-by-step, problem-solving, procedure for calculations. It contains well-defined instructions for calculating a function in a finite number of steps.

Align – Arranging in a straight line. Parallel.

Aliquot Part – An aliquot part is an integer that is an exact divisor, or factor, of a quantity. 6 is an aliquot part of 24.

Alternate Angle – Alternate angles are two angles on opposite sides of a transversal line that cuts two lines. Both angles are either interior or exterior to the two lines.

Alternate Exterior Angles – The pairs of angles on opposite sides of the transversal line (The line that crosses two lines) and are outside of the two lines.

Alternate Interior Angles - The pairs of angles on opposite sides of the transversal line (The line that crosses two lines) and are inside of the two lines.

Alternating Group – A group of permutations (the rearranging of objects) of a finite set consisting of all possibilities of a given number of items.

Altitude – Altitude is the measure of the perpendicular distance from the base to the opposite vertex. Altitude is the "height" when calculating the area of a triangle. Also, in parallel lines, the altitude is the measure, the perpendicular distance, from the base to the opposite side.

AM – It's a Latin word that means anno mundi. It starts at midnight, 12:00 A.M., and ends at noon, 12:00 P.M.

Amount – The total sum of two or more quantities, or sums. The sum, the total, and the quantity are all examples of amount.

Analog Clock – A time device, a clock, or watch that has moving hands that show you the time.

Analog Gadgets – Analog is a continuous transmission of information, whereas digital gadgets, or devices, read only zeros and ones.

Angle – An angle is two rays that move away from a common endpoint, which is called the vertex.

Angle of Reflection – The angle made by a ray reflected from a surface and a line perpendicular to the surface at the point of reflection.

Angle of Rotation – The measure of degrees that a figure is rotated about a fixed point.

Angular Distance – Angular distance is the angular separation (distance) between two objects, or points, as perceived by the onlooker.

Annual, Annually – An annual event is one that occurs, or recurs, once per year.

Annual Percentage Rate (APR) – The yearly rate that is charged for borrowing, expressed as a percentage, that represents the actual yearly cost of monies over the period (timeframe) of a loan.

Annulus – The area between two coplanar concentric circles (a flat ring-shaped object).

Anticlockwise – Counterclockwise (The hands on a clock going backwards).

Antiparallel – Being parallel but going in opposite directions.

Apex – An apex is the highest point, or vertex.

Apothem – The distance from the center of a regular polygon to the midpoint of a side. Apothem is also the distance from the center of a circle to the midpoint of a chord.

Approximate / Approximation – Approximation is not exact, but very close to the actual. The approximation of pi is 3.14.

Arbelos – A Greek word for a "shoemaker's knife" that was used to cut and trim leather. Arbelos is constrained by three semi-circles. Take one-half circle with diameter AB, and place two smaller circles inside with diameters AC and CB. The sum of the two smaller arc lengths equals the larger.

Arc (of the Circle) – An arc is a portion of the circumference of a circle, and sometimes that of an ellipse. Take a slice of pizza, no matter the size, and measuring the length of the crust. The length of the crust would be the arc.

Area – Area is the number of square units that cover a surface; it's the amount of space of the surface inside the boundary of a flat area, which can be any size or shape.

Area of a Circle – Area equals pi times the radius squared. Area = $\pi \times r^2$

Area of a Parallelogram – Area equals the base times the altitude (height). Area = $b \times h$

Area of a Ring – Area equals pi times (radius 1 squared minus radius two squared). Area = $\pi \times (r_1^2 - r_2^2)$

Area of a Sector – Area equals 1/2 times the radius squared times the angle in radians. Area = $1/2 \times r^2 \times °$

Area of a Square or Rectangle – Area equals length times the width. Area = $l \times w$ (a square could also be s^2)

Area of a Trapezoid – Area equals 1/2(a+b) times the height. Area = $1/2 \times (b_1 + b_2) \times h$

Area of a Triangle – Area equals 1/2 of the base times height (altitude). Area = $1/2 \times b \times h$; the sum of the measures of the angles of a triangle equals 180°

Area of an Ellipse – Area equals pi times a times b. Area = $\pi \times a \times b$

Areal Coordinates – The location of a point is specified by the areas of the component regions. Areal coordinates are also known as barycentric coordinates coefficients in the representation of a point in a simplex as a linear combination of the vertices of the simplex.

Argument – An input to that of a function. An argument is a variable that affects the result of the function.

Arithmetic – The mathematics of integers, complex numbers, rational numbers, or real numbers, using the basic operations of adding, subtracting, multiplying, and dividing.

Arithmetic Sequence – Arithmetic sequence is a sequence where the difference between consecutive numbers is the same. It's a sequence of numbers that has a constant between every two consecutive terms, in which each term except the first term is the result of adding, or subtracting, the same number to the preceding term. For the arithmetic sequence 1, 4, 7, 10…, three is added to each number in the sequence.

Arms of an Angle – Arms of an angle are any of the two straight lines that form the angle.

Array – A systematic arrangement of objects that are placed in proper or desired order. Arrays are usually arranged in rows and columns.

Ascending Order – Increasing and arranged from smallest to largest. 2, 5, 6, 15, 50, or, A, B, C, M, Z

Asset – Assets are items of ownership with economic value that can be liquidated to cash, such as a house or car.

Associative Law – When adding or multiplying, grouping the numbers in any way will provide the same result.

Associative Property of Addition – Adding a set of numbers will result in the same answer no matter how the numbers are grouped. The numbers in the parenthesis, the associative property, are considered one group, or unit. (8 + 3) + 4 = 15; 8 + (3 + 4) = 15

Associative Property of Multiplication - Multiplying a set of numbers will result in the same answer no matter how the numbers are grouped. The numbers in the parenthesis, the associative property, are considered one group, or unit. (3 x 2) x 8 = 48; 3 x (2 x 8) = 48

Asymmetry – Asymmetry is the lacking, or absence, of symmetry.

Asymptote – Asymptote is a line or curve that approaches a given curve, or graph, rather closely, but never touches, or intersects, it.

Attribute – An attribute is a characteristic or a property of a person or object; shape, size, or color.

Average (Mean) – The average is the sum of the items in a set of data divided by the number of items. To calculate an average, take all the numbers (members) in a given data set and add them together. Then, divide by how many numbers (members) there are in the data set. The average, or mean, of the data set: 1, 2, 5, 6, and 21 = 7. 1 + 2 + 5 + 6 + 21 = 35. 35 (the total number by adding all the data set members together) divided by 5 (the number of members in the data set) equals 7.

Axes – The plural form of axis. Axes are the two number lines that form a coordinate plane. The horizontal number line is the x-axis, and the vertical number line is the y-axis.

Axiom Schema – Axiom schema is a formula in the language of an axiomatic system in which one or more schematic variables appear. These schematic variables represent any term, or sub formula, of the system and may or may not be required to satisfy certain conditions.

Axis (Geometry) – An axis is an imaginary line around which something rotates.

Axis (Graph) – An axis is also one of the reference lines in a coordinate system. The horizontal (X-axis) and vertical (Y-axis) lines that make up the quadrants of a coordinate plane, used to plot numbers.

Axis of Symmetry – The axis of symmetry is a line through a shape, or object, which displays a mirror image, or reflection to that of the other side. Both halves will be identical if the shape, or object, is folded in half along the axis of symmetry.

B – Balance through Breadth

Balance – To balance is to have the same mass or quantity on both sides. Balance is an equal distribution of weight.

Bank – A bank is a financial institution that offers loans which require payback, with interest. It also watches after people's money, paying interest for the use of the money.

Bankrupt – Bankrupt is the inability to repay a debt, or debts. In order for a bankruptcy to take place it must be legally declared by a bankruptcy court. Other than basic things, such as a house or car, the person loses just about everything. Their credit rating is destroyed and they likely will not be able to secure a loan again for years.

Bar Graph – A bar graph is a graph that uses either vertical or horizontal bars to visually represent data, or values. The higher or the longer the bar extends, the greater the value.

Bar Notation – In decimals, bar notation is a bar that is used above a number, or numbers, to identify a repeating pattern, or digits.

Base (Geometry) – The bottom line of a shape or plane. The base is also the bottom face of a solid, the part of the solid that stands on the surface of another object.

Base Numbers – The base is the number that is multiplied by itself by the number of times, as determined by the exponent (index). Five to the third power, written 5^3, would be expressed 5 x 5 x 5 = 125. Our number system is a base 10 system, or decimal number system. Each place value, ones, tens, hundreds, thousands, etc. has ten units, or digits.

Base Ten Blocks – Base ten blocks are math manipulative blocks that show base 10 number values. One (1) three-dimensional block is called a "short." Ten (10) three-dimensional blocks stacked on top of one another is called a "long." One hundred (100) three-dimensional blocks stacked ten high and ten wide, 10 x 10, is called a "flat." One thousand (1,000) three-dimensional blocks stacked ten high, ten wide, and ten deep (looks like a cube), 10 x 10 x 10, is called a "block."

Basic Facts – Basic facts are one digit numbers that are used when adding, subtracting, multiplying, and dividing. 5 + 3 = 8 is an addition fact. 3 – 3 = 0 is a subtraction fact. 9 x 8 = 72 is a multiplication fact (the two factors are the single units). 16 ÷ 4 = 4 is a division fact (the divisor and the quotient are the single units).

Benchmark Angles – Benchmark angles are reference angles that are used to help determine, or assist with, other angles. 45°, 90°, and 180° are common reference angles.

Bi – Bi is a prefix that means two, or twice. A bicycle has two wheels. The binary number system, used in computers and digital media, uses only two numbers, zero and one.

Billion – A billion contains a one, followed by nine (9) zeros. A billion ($1,000,000,000) dollars can create one thousand millionaires.

Binary – This number system is made up solely of zeros and ones. It is used in computers and digital media.

Binary System – To represent numbers, powers of 10 are used in the decimal system, the system we most commonly use. The binary system on the other hand, used in computers and digital media, uses in a similar manner the powers of 2 and is written using the digits zero and one, to express each number.

Binomial – A binomial is a polynomial that has two terms, 6x + 2y; x + 16; 2xy - 3

Bisect – To divide, or cut, in two equal halves (parts). You can bisect an angle or a line.

Bisector – The "line" that divides, or cuts, the angle or line in two equal halves (parts).

Bivariate Data – Data that contains two variables that are usually related in some way. A scatter plot is often used to visually determine if there is a relationship, if any, between the two variables. Test scores in relation to studying is an example of bivariate data.

Block - A block represents 1,000 three-dimensional blocks. Math manipulative blocks that show base 10 numbers values. One (1) three-dimensional block is called a "short." Ten (10) three-dimensional blocks stacked on top of one another is called a "long." One hundred (100) three-dimensional blocks stacked ten high and ten wide, 10 x 10, is called a "flat." One thousand (1,000) three-dimensional blocks stacked ten high, ten wide, and ten deep (looks like a cube), 10 x 10 x 10, is called a "block."

Bond – Usually from government or a business, a bond is a certificate that states how much money was loaned and the terms regarding the interest amount and the payback due date. Generally, a bond is very much like a loan, or mortgage.

Boundary – A boundary defines the area or space of an object. The boundary is the border, or line, around the outside (exterior) of a shape, also called the perimeter.

Box – As a two-dimensional rectangular shape, a box has a length and a width. As a three-dimensional object, a box has a length a width, and a height.

Box and Whisker Plot (Box Plot) – A box and whisker plot shows the distribution of a set of data using a diagram, or graph. The maximum and minimum values of the data (sometimes referred to as the "range"), the upper and lower quartiles (called the interquartile range), and the median (the middle number in the data set) are displayed within a box and whisker plot.

Brackets – Brackets are symbols that are used to group things together in mathematical expressions. (12 + 5) – (4 x 2) = 9. Brackets used can be of the following: ( ); { }; [ ]; < >

Breadth – Breadth is the width of an object. Breadth is the side to side measurement of an object, usually the shorter side of a rectangle.

C – Calandar through Cylinder

Calandar – A calendar is a table, diagram, or chart that displays the year, months, weeks, and days.

Calculate – Calculate is to labor an answer to a problem, usually through basic math operations, such as adding, subtracting, multiplying, and/or dividing.

Calculator – A calculator is a machine (computer) or program that performs mathematical operations.

Capacity – Capacity is the amount that something, such as a container, can hold. Regarding mathematical terms, capacity is usually measured in volume, pints, gallons, liters, and milliliters.

Cardinal Number – Numbers that say how many number of items there are in a set. The items will be counted in order such as one, two, three, four, and five…

Carroll Diagram – The Carroll Diagram is named after the mathematician, Lewis Carroll. A Carroll diagram allows the sorting of numbers that can be categorized as even, not even, a multiple of four, not a multiple of four, etc.

Cartesian Coordinates – Cartesian coordinates provide a way to identify the position of a location on a graph or map. One common way is with the use of a Cartesian or coordinate plane where the location is pinpointed on a grid via a horizontal x-axis and a vertical y-axis.

Cartesian (Coordinate) Plane – The horizontal x-axis and the vertical y-axis of a grid intersect at a point called the origin, (0,0). The x-axis location is always listed first and the y-axis location is always listed second. The Cartesian plane is broken up into four quadrants and is used to identify the position of a location, such as (0,-3), (2,4), (-3,-2), (-1,0), etc.

Categorical Data – Categorical data is a statistical term that categorizes in words, qualitative data, rather than numbers, quantitative data. An example of a categorical data chart might be sports games, and it could be represented through a bar graph, or chart. The categories could be baseball, football, basketball, soccer, etc. and the height or length of the bars on the chart would reference the indicated sport.

Celsius (°C) – Celsius is a metric system scale that measures temperature. Water freezes at 0° C (32° F). Water boils at 100° C (212° F). Celsius is also referred to as centigrade.

Census – Rather than gathering a sample, a census is a complete collection of data from the entire population. The US census is taken every ten years to determine the exact number of people in the United States.

Cent – A cent equals one penny. One-hundred pennies make up a dollar. The prefix "cent" equals one-hundred. A century is one-hundred years.

Center – The center falls directly in the middle of something.

Center of Rotation – The center of rotation is the point around which an object is rotated.

Centi – Centi is a prefix that means 1/100 (one-hundredth).

Centigrade – See also the term Celsius. This thermometer was invented by Anders Celsius, a Swedish astronomer, in 1742.

Centimeter (cm) – A centimeter is a metric unit for measuring length. A centimeter is 1/100 (one-hundredth) of a meter. One US inch equals 2.54 centimeters.

Central Angle – The central angle is the angle formed at the center of a circle by two given points on the circle. As the points change, so does the central angle, which will be 180° or smaller.

Centroid- Centroid is the point where the three line segments of a triangle intersects.

Century – A century equals one-hundred years.

Certain – In mathematical probability, the likelihood of an outcome, or desired result, is measured on a scale, ranging from 0 to 1. If the conclusion is 0, the outcome is impossible; there is 0% chance that the occurrence will happen. If the conclusion is 1, the outcome is said to be "certain" to happen; there is 100% chance that the occurrence will happen. There is an even 50% chance of the occurrence happening if the scale measures 0.5.

Chance – The likelihood that a particular outcome, or event, will occur. See the term, "Certain."

Chord – A chord is a straight line that joins two endpoints on the circumference of a circle, or a straight line that joins two endpoints on a curve.

Circle – A circle is a shape that is two-dimensional and has an unbroken line (curve) that is continuously the same distance from the center. It is the set of all points at a given distance (the radius) from a fixed point (the center).

Circumference – The circumference is the distance around the edge of a circle, or any shape that is curved. The circumference of a circle is related to that of a square's or triangle's perimeter, which is the total measurement of the sides. The formula is: Circumference = 2 x π x r

Circumradius – A polygon within a circle, circumradius is the radius to each of the vertices, the corner points of the polygon.

Class Interval – Class interval is a subdivision within a range of values. An example would be yearly rainfall for the years 2007 through 2011. Each year would then be broken down into quarterly, or monthly, rainfall within each year. The broken down quarterly, or monthly, rainfall would be the class interval.

Classify – The arranging of objects, shapes, numbers, etc. in groups.

Clockwise – Clockwise is like that of a clock. All three hands, second, minute, hour, move forward, or clockwise.

Closed Curve – A closed curve is a curved line that is joined to both its starting and ending points. There are no end points.

Closed Interval – Closed interval is part of a straight line that includes its endpoints.

Cluster – A cluster is numbers (data) which tend to gather around a particular point in a set of values. For the numbers, 2, 6, 9, 10, 14, 16, 19, 19, 20, 21, 22, 27, 30, the cluster is around the number 20.

Coalition – A coalition is a set of its elements, with no specific order. The set cannot be an empty set.

Coefficient – A coefficient is a number which multiplies a variable. For $5y + 6$, the 5 is the coefficient.

Coincident – Coincident is a shape or line that lies precisely on the top of the other one.

Collateral – Collateral is something of value used, such as a house or car that a borrower will forfeit if he cannot pay back the lender.

Collinear Points – Collinear points are three or more points that lie on the same straight line.

Column – A column is an organization of numbers, or values that are one above the other. The numbers are arranged vertically. In Microsoft Excel, the columns are A, B, C, D, etc.

Column Graph – A column graph uses bars to show quantities or numbers so they can be easily compared. Another name for a column graph is a bar graph.

Combination – A combination is a collection of "stuff" (a group of items) that is chosen from within a group of items where the order doesn't matter. If you have 8 shirts, 6 ties, and 5 pairs of pants, how many combinations can you make? ($8 \times 6 \times 5 = 240$ combinations)

Commission – Commission is usually paid as a percentage, a commission is a fee paid for a service. A realtor earned a 1.5% commission on the house she sold for $100,000. Her commission was $1,500.

Common Denominator – A common denominator is when the denominator (bottom number) is the same number for all of the fractions. With the denominator, a number (the same number) must be able to divide into all the denominators evenly, with no remainders.

Common Difference – In a series of numbers, the common difference is the same between each number. For the numbers, 1, 2, 3, 4, and 5, the common difference is 1. For the numbers, 3, 6, 9, 12, and 15, the common difference is 3.

Common Factor – A common factor is a number (a whole number) that is a factor (divides into two or more other numbers evenly, without a remainder) of two or more numbers. 6 is a common factor of 24, 42, and 600.

Common Multiple – A common multiple is a multiple that is shared by two or more numbers. 20 is a multiple of 4 and 5 (4 x 5). 20 is a multiple of 2 and 10 (2 x 10). 20 is a multiple of 1 and 20 (1 x 20). Therefore, 20 is a common multiple of 1, 2, 4, 5, 10, and 20.

Commutative Law – When adding and multiplying, the numbers can be calculated in any order to arrive at the same answer. 2 + 3 + 8 = 8 + 2 + 3; (5 x 3) x 2 = (2 x 3) x 5

Commutative Property of Addition - When adding, the numbers can be calculated in any order to arrive at the same answer. (5 + 9) + 15 = 29 = 9 + (15 + 5)

Commutative Property of Multiplication - When multiplying, the numbers can be calculated in any order to arrive at the same answer. (1 x 7) x 6 = 42 = 1 x (6 x 7)

Compass – A compass is a device (instrument) that displays the direction one is traveling; N, NE, NW, S, SE, SW, E, W.

Compass (Drawing) – A compass is an instrument that draws arcs or circles. A pencil is inserted into one end. The pointed end of the compass is placed at the center of the circle. The measurement (radius of the circle) is selected. Setting the measure at 2" will create a circle with a 2" radius and a 4" diameter.

Complement – In probability, the event and its complement make up all of the possible outcomes. If a spinner is numbered 1 through 8 and an 8 is spun, the event is 8. The complement is 1, 2, 3, 4, 5, 6, and 7. Therefore, the complement is the numbers not part of the event.

Complementary Angles – Complementary angles are two angles added together to equal 90°, or a right angle. A 55° angle plus a 35° angle is 90°. These two angles form a right angle, and are complementary angles.

Complex Numbers – Complex numbers are a mixture of real (1, 3.75, -8) and imaginary ($\sqrt{-1}$, square root of minus one) numbers.

Composite Numbers – Composite numbers are numbers that have more than two factors (other than 1 and itself). 10 is a composite number. Its factors are 1, 2, 5, and 10. 13, 19, and 23 are not composite numbers. Their only factors are 1 and itself. These numbers are called prime numbers.

Compound Interest – Compound interest is interest that is compounded at specified intervals (daily, monthly, quarterly, semi-annually, or annually) and added to the principal at the end of the interval. In other words, compound interest earns interest on both principal and interest. The interest is compounded with the principal. Year 1, $10,000 is earning interest. Let's say $500 was earned in interest. Year 2, $10,500 is earning interest. Let's say $525 was earned in interest. Year 3, $11,025 is earning interest, and so on.

Computation – Computation is using logic or mathematical operations to find an answer to a problem.

Concave – A polygon, or object, that curves inwards.

Concentric Circles – Concentric circles are circles that have the same center point, but are of different sizes (the circles).

Concurrent Lines – Concurrent lines are two or more lines that intersect at the same point.

Cone – A cone is a solid three-dimensional shape with an elliptical or circular base, which has a curved surface and tapers to a single point. The point is the vertex.

Congruent – Something that is congruent has the same shape and size. If the shape, or shapes, can fit precisely on the other(s), they are said to be congruent.

Conic Section – Slicing through a cone and taking a section from it is a conic section. Doing this will create a circle, an ellipse, a hyperbola, or a parabola.

Conjugate – Conjugate is changing the sign inside two terms. For 5y – 3, the conjugate is 5y + 3.

Consecutive – Numbers which follow each other in order. There are no disruptions, or unbroken sequences. 1, 2, 3, 4, and 5 are consecutive integers. 5.5, 5.6, 5.7, 5.8, and 5.9 are consecutive rational numbers.

Consecutive Interior Angles – When the transversal line crosses two lines, the consecutive interior angles are the inside of the two lines on either side of the transversal line.

Constant – A constant is a term or quantity that has a fixed value that doesn't change or contain a variable. For 5y + 6 = 26, the 6 and 26 are the constants.

Constructible Numbers – Taking the lengths of line segments that are erected with a ruler, or straightedge, and by using a compass, all rational numbers and positive integers are constructible, in addition to, the square roots of said numbers.

Continuous Data – Within a selected range, continuous data can take on any value and have an infinite number of possibilities. An example would be yearly rainfall for the year 2011. January through December would be the selected range (Discrete Data). Rainfall for each month takes on any measurable value and has an infinite number of possibilities, therefore, Continuous Data.

Convergent – Convergent is a sequence of numbers, or objects, that approaches towards the same point, or value. Counting to 100 is convergent. The converging numbers 1, 2, 3, 4…100 all head toward the same value, 100.

Converging Lines – An object, or something, that heads toward the same point. Four people are standing at each corner of a basketball court. They all begin to move toward the center of the court and meet there. Their paths are converging lines.

Conversion Graph – Usually displayed as a line graph, a conversion graph converts one unit of measurement to another. An example would be inches represented by the x-axis and centimeters represented by the y-axis. The lines would intersect at 1 inch = 2.54 centimeters.

Conversions – 60 seconds = 1 minute; 60 minutes = 1 hour; 24 hours = 1 day; 7 days = 1 week; 30 days = 1 month; 52 weeks = 1 year; 12 inches = 1 foot; 3 feet = 1 yard; 36 inches = 1 yard; 5,280 feet = 1 mile; 1,760 yards = 1 mile; 10 millimeters = 1 centimeter; 100 centimeters = 1 meter; 1,000 meters = 1 kilometer; 8 fluid ounces = 1 cup; 2 cups = 1 pint; 2 pints = 1 quart; 4 quarts = 1 gallon; 1,000 milliliters (mL) = 1 liter (L); 16 ounces = 1 pound; 2,000 pounds = 1 ton; 1,000 milligrams = 1 gram; 100 centigrams = 1 gram; 10 grams = 1 dekagram; 1,000 grams = 1 kilogram

Convex - A polygon, or object, that curves outwards.

Coordinate Plane – A coordinate plane is the plane that contains both the x-axis and the y-axis. These two axes are perpendicular to each other and intersect at the point of origin, or (0, 0).

Coordinates – Coordinates are sets of values that point to a specific location on the coordinate plane. For (2, -3), the 2 represents the horizontal x-axis, always the first number, and the -3 represents the vertical y–axis, always the second number.

Coplanar – Geometric objects that lie on the same, or a common, plane.

Coprime – Two integers that have no common factors.

Corner – A corner is the vertex, or the point where surfaces meet.

Corresponding Angles – When the transversal line crosses two lines, the corresponding angles are the angles found in the same position. Four corresponding angles will be created when the transversal line crosses two lines.

Cosecant (csc) – The cosecant of an angle, which is found in a right triangle, is the hypotenuse (the "C" side or the slope) divided by the opposite side of the hypotenuse. It is equal to 1/sine.

Cosine (cos) - The cosine of an angle, which is found in a right triangle, is the adjacent side (of the hypotenuse, the "C" side or slope) divided by the hypotenuse.

Cotangent - The cotangent of an angle, which is found in a right triangle, is the adjacent side divided by the opposite side.

Counterclockwise - Like that opposite of a clock. The hands move backward, or counterclockwise.

Counting Number – Used to count or order things, a counting number is 1, 2, 3, 4, 5… to forever, or infinity. A counting number is not 0, and it contains no negative numbers, decimals, or fractions.

Counting Principle – The counting principle is the number of outcomes for an event. Usually used when figuring probability, the counting principle is a method, using multiplication, to work out the total outcomes, or possibilities, by multiplying the number of items in each leg of the event. If we have 5 different pairs of pants, 8 different shirts, and 3 ties, we could create 120 different clothing combinations. We multiply 5 x 8 x 3.

Credit – Credit is borrowing money, usually to purchase something, from a creditor with the intent to pay the lender of the money back, with interest.

Cross Multiply – With two proportionate fractions, multiplying the numerator of the first fraction with the denominator of the second fraction will equal multiplying the denominator of the first fraction with the numerator of the second fraction. The equation such that a/b = c/d, when cross-multiplied, will be ad = bc. The result equals 1, when simplified. For the fractions 3/4 = 12/16, we get 48 = 48 when these proportions are cross-multiplied. This fraction, 48/48 would be reduced to 1.

Cross-Section – When cutting through a solid object, the cross-section is the view of the surface (the face) that is seen.

Cube – A die, or dice, is a cube. A cube (a solid that looks like a square box) is a rectangular prism that has 6 equal square faces, 12 edges, and 8 vertices (points). A cube is also one of the platonic solids.

Cubed Number (x^3) – A cubed number is multiplying a number by itself three times. A cubed number is raising the number to the third power. 6^3 = 6 x 6 x 6 = 216.

Cubed Root ($3\sqrt{}$) – A cubed root is three matching factors of a number that is the product of those factors. 4^3 = 64. Therefore, the cubed root of 64 = 4 (4 x 4 x 4)

Cubic Centimeter (cm^3) – A cubic centimeter is a three-dimensional object that measures (metric system) volume. A cubic centimeter measures 1 centimeter (cm) on each of the 12 edges. The symbol is cm^3.

Cubic Measure (x^3) – Measures the capacity or the volume of an object, or liquid. A cube that measures 5 inches would equal 125 cubic inches. 5 x 5 x 5 = 125. In other words, 125 one inch cubes would fit inside a cube that measures 5 inches long, 5 inches wide, and 5 inches high.

Cubic Meter (m^3) - A cubic meter is a three-dimensional object that measures (metric system) volume. A cubic meter measures 1 meter (m) on each of the 12 edges.

Cuboid – A cuboid is a rectangular box-shaped object that has 6 sides (faces), 12 edges, and 8 vertices (points).

Cumulative Frequency – Cumulative frequency is a running total of frequencies. If there are 5 pennies, 8 nickels, 4 dimes, and 3 quarters, the total frequencies equal 20.

Curve – A curve is a line that is not straight.

Cylinder – A cylinder is a solid shape (three-dimensional) with one curved side and two identical (congruent) parallel circular, or elliptical, bases.

D – Data through Dozen

Data – Data is a gathering of numerical information, such as values, facts, or measurements. The information is typically collected through measuring, questioning, or observation, and displayed through charts or graphs.

Date – The date is a record showing the precise month, day, and year. Today is December 31, 2011.

Deca – Deca is a prefix that means 10.

Decade – A decade is a time period equivalent to 10 years.

Decagon – A decagon is a flat-shaped polygon that has 10 straight sides.

Decahedron – A decahedron is a three-dimensional solid shape with 10 flat faces.

Decimal – A decimal is based on the number 10 (better known as the base 10 system). Regarding place value, all the numbers to the right of the decimal have a value that is less than one. $1.30 has the 3 (valued at 30 cents) to the right of the decimal, and is valued at less than 1 dollar.

Decimal Fraction – A decimal fraction is a fraction that is written as a decimal. 1/4 = 0.25

Decimal Number System – The decimal number system is a number system based on the number 10. This system is also known as the base 10 system and it is the number system that we use.

Decimal Point – A decimal point is a point (dot) that separates whole numbers (the whole) and decimal fractions (the part). In money, the decimal point separates dollars and cents.

Decrease – To decrease is to reduce or to get smaller in number or in size.

Deduct – Deduct is to subtract or to take away from something else.

Deficient Number - A number such that the sum of all its divisors (factors), not including itself, is smaller than the number itself Example: Fifteen (15) is a deficient number. The factors of 15, not including itself, are 1, 3, and 5. This equals 9, which is smaller than 15. Twenty (20) is not a deficient number. The factors of 20, not including itself, are 1, 2, 4, 5, and 10. This equals 22, which is not smaller than 20. The first twenty deficient numbers are 1, 2, 3, 4, 5, 7, 8, 9, 10, 11, 13, 14, 15, 16, 17, 19, 21, 22, 23, and 25 (also see abundant numbers)

Degree (Angles) – A degree is a measurement that measures the size of an angle. In a full circle, or complete rotation, there are 360°. A right angle is 90° and a straight angle (line) is 180°.

Degree (Temperature) – Degree "°" is a measurement of temperature in degrees Fahrenheit or degrees Celsius. Water freezes at 32° and boils at 212° Fahrenheit. Water freezes at 0° and boils at 100° Celsius,

Denominator – The denominator is the bottom number in a fraction and represents an equal number of parts that something (the whole) is divided into. The pizza has been cut into six equal parts. The number of slices, in this case six, is the denominator. The denominator can also be used on the right side, separated by the division symbol, such as 5 / 6. The six (6) is the denominator.

Density – Density is the amount of matter in an object. A 2" x 3" x 6" piece of wood is more dense (contains more matter) than a 2" x 3" x 6" piece of Styrofoam. A 1" diameter 18" long lead pipe is denser than a 1" diameter 18" long solid iron pipe. The lead pipe contains more matter, and therefore, has more mass than the iron pipe.

Dependent Events – A dependent event is an outcome (or occurrence) that is affected by prior outcomes and may also affect the probability of the event. If there are twenty names in a hat and one of the names is yours, each time a name is drawn provides a better chance that the next name drawn will be yours.

Descending Order - Decreasing and arranged from largest to smallest.
50, 15, 6, 5, 2, or, Z, M, C, B, A

Diagonal – A diagonal is a straight line that joins two non-adjacent corners (vertices) of a polygon. The line has to be within the shape, not along one of its edges.

Diagram – A diagram is a simplified plan, sketch, or drawing that describes or clarifies something through appearances or structures, explaining how something works or how to assemble it.

Diameter – The diameter is a straight line (chord) that goes through the center of a circle. It connects two points on the outer edge (the circumference) of the circle.

Diamond – A diamond (also called a rhombus) is a parallelogram with four equal sides and equal opposite angles.

Dice – Dice is the plural form of Die.

Die – A die is a solid object (usually a cube) with numbers, letters, or dots. A die (or dice) provides a random number, or outcome, when rolled. A die (dice) is usually used when playing games.

Difference – The difference is the result of subtracting one number from another number. The difference between 30 and 23 is 7.

Difference of Squares - The difference is the result of subtracting one squared number from another squared number. The difference between 4^2 (16) and 2^2 (4) is 12.

Digit – A digit is a symbol used to show a number. The four digit number 1,357 is represented by the digits one, three, five, and seven.

Digital Clock - A time device, a clock, or watch that has numerals (no moving hands) to show you the time.

Dilation – Dilation is to take something, such as an object or shape, and resize (widen) it, making it larger. By using dilation, the picture was enlarged from 2" x 3" to 4" x 6".

Dimension – Dimension is a measurement of length and refers to length, breadth (width), and height (altitude).

Directed Number – A directed number is a negative or positive number and usually has the sign in front of it (positive numbers don't always place the "+" sign in front of it). -8, -12, +1, +15, and +1,000 are all examples of directed numbers.

Direction – Direction is the line or course on which something is going, or pointing. I am traveling South on Interstate 95.

Discount – A discount is a reduction in price, value, or quantity (from the original price, value, or quantity). The regular price of an item is $25.00. A 10% discount would reduce the cost by $2.50, therefore resulting in a discounted final price of $22.50.

Discrete Data - Discrete data can only have a finite or limited number of possibilities. An example would be yearly rainfall for the year 2011. January through December would be the selected range, or the Discrete Data. The actual rainfall for each month can take on any measurable value and has an infinite number of possibilities, or Continuous Data.

Displacement (Distance) – Displacement is how far something is from the start once it has finished. If the distance from point A to point B is 6 miles, and the distance from point B to point C is 10 miles, the distance, or displacement, from point A (the starting point) to point C (the ending point) is 11.7 miles.

Displacement (Fluid) – Displacement is how much fluid is pushed away when an object is completely submerged in it. The object is placed in the liquid and it will displace its own volume, causing the water level to rise.

Distance – The measurement in length between point A and point B. Distances are commonly measured in centimeters (cm), inches (in.), feet (ft.), meters (m), yards (yd.), kilometers (km), and miles (mi.). The formula for distance is: Distance = Rate x Time

Distributive Property (Law) – The Distributive Property states that the product of a number and a sum is equal to the sum of the individual products of addends and the number. $a(b + c) = ab + ac$ Example: $5(2 + 4) = 30 = 5(2) + 5(4) = 10 + 20 = 30$.

Divide (Division) – Division ($\div$ or /) is sharing or grouping a number into equal parts. There are 28 people that will be placed into groups of 4. How many groups will there be? $28 \div 4 = 7$. There will be 7 equal groups.

Dividend – The dividend is the number that is being divided. For the problem $15 \div 3 = 5$, 15 is the dividend.

Divisible – A number is divisible when that number, divided by another number, results in a whole number, with no remainder. For the problem 36÷12=3, 36 is divisible by 12. 12 goes into 36 three times evenly. There is no remainder.

Divisor – The divisor is the number that is "divided by." For the problem (fifteen "divided by" three) 15 ÷ 3 = 5, 3 is the divisor.

Dodecagon – A dodecagon is a polygon (flat-shaped) that comprises of 12 straight sides.

Dodecahedron – A dodecahedron, a flat-sided, solid polyhedron, has 12 faces. Think of a 12-sided dice. A dodecahedron is one of the platonic solids.

Dollar – A dollar ($) is 100 cents. 2 halves, 4 quarters, 10 dimes, 20 nickels, and 100 pennies all make up one dollar.

Domain of a Function – The domain of a function is the values (all of them) that go into a function.

Dot Plot – Using a number line that represents a population (sample), one dot is used (and is placed on the corresponding number) for each member of the sample. The dots are stacked up if more than one dot represents the same number. If test scores are 80, 81, 85, 86, 86, and 89, a dot plot could range from 80 to 90. Each score would have one dot on it except for the score of 86. It would consist of two dots.

Double – Double is twice as large. Adding the same number twice or multiplying a number by two will double a number. 15 + 15 = 30. 15 x 2 = 30.

Dozen – A dozen equals 12 of something. A carton of eggs contain one dozen eggs.

E – Eccentricity through Exterior Angle

Eccentricity – Eccentricity deals with conic sections and their variations (or deviations) from being perfect circles, which have a 0 eccentricity.

Edge – The edge is where two surfaces join, or intersect. An edge is also a shape's boundary; it's the intersection of faces of a polyhedron.

Element – An element is a member of a set. With the set of even numbers, {2,4,6,8,10,12,14,…}, 8 is an element of this set.

Ellipse – An ellipse (a conic section or cross-section of a cone) is oval in shape. It looks like a flattened circle. Earth travels around the sun in an elliptical, or slightly oval, orbit.

Endpoint – An endpoint is a point that marks either end of a line segment.

Enlarge – To make bigger, or larger. The photograph will be enlarged from 4"x6" to 8"x12."

Equal – Being equal is to have the exact value, or to have the same amount of something. I have 4 quarters; you have 5 dimes and 10 nickels. We both have an equal amount of money, $1.00.

Equal Sign – The equal sign is represented by "="

Equality – Equality means to have the same value; being equal

Equate – Equate is to make equal or to treat as an equivalent

Equation – An equation is a mathematical statement that uses symbols and contains an equal "=" sign to show that two expressions are equal, or are the same. $5 \times 4 = 18 + 2$

Equation of a Straight Line – Equation of a straight line consists of plugging in data to see if it satisfies the equation. On the coordinate plane, the coordinates are (-3, -1). Does this satisfy the equation $y = x + 2$? Plugging in the numbers results in $-1 = -3 + 2$. Simplifying this statement results in $-1 = -1$. This equation is satisfied.

Equiangular – Equiangular is to have all the angles equal to one another. An equilateral triangle has three angles, all 60°. A square or rectangle has four right angles, all 90°.

Equilateral Triangle – An equilateral triangle has three equal (congruent) sides (the same length), in addition to, three equal (congruent) angles, all 60°.

Equinox – The equinox (spring and fall) happens twice a year. This is when every area on the Earth experiences exactly 12 hours of daylight and 12 hours of darkness.

Equivalent – Equivalent means to have the same value. 5,280 feet is equivalent (equal) to 1 mile.

Equivalent Fractions – Equivalent fractions are fractions that have the same value. 1 = 16/16; 3/5 = 6/10 = 12/20.

Error of Measurement – Error of measurement is the difference between a measured or computed value (in other words, an estimate) versus a theoretically "exact" value. This candidate has a 52% approval rating with an error of measurement (or margin of error) of +/- 3%.

Estimate – To estimate is to make a rough approximation (guess) or calculation, and it is usually concluded by a rounded figure. Seeing a full parking lot with about 50 cars wide and 20 cars deep gives me an estimated guess that there are 1,000 cars in the parking lot.

Evaluate – To evaluate is to work out a problem; solving it by finding a numerical value to answer the problem, or question. $2x + 5 = 13$; $x = 4$

Even Number – An even number is a number that can be divided by 2 that doesn't have a remainder. All even numbers end with 2, 4, 6, 8, or 0. Examples include: -156, -4, 0, 22, 48, and 1,000,000.

Event – In statistics, an event is the outcome or group of outcomes of the sample space.

Expanded Notation – Expanded notation is a way of writing numbers to illustrate place value (the value of each digit). $56{,}495 = 5 \times 10{,}000 + 6 \times 1{,}000 + 4 \times 100 + 9 \times 10 + 5$

Exponent – The exponent (also called the index, power of, or raised) dictates the number of times that the base number is multiplied by itself. Six squared, $6^2 = 6 \times 6 = 36$; five cubed, $5^3 = 5 \times 5 \times 5 = 125$. The six and the five are the bases and the exponents are the ^{2} (pronounced squared) and the ^{3} (pronounced cubed).

Expression – An expression is a single number or grouped together numbers, symbols, and/or operators that show value and that represent a quantity or a number. 6×8, $3x^3$, $(5 \times 2 + 9)$, 7, and $2y-3$ are all examples of expressions.

Exterior Angle – An exterior angle is the angle that exists when one side of a polygon is extended. The exterior angle is the angle outside of the polygon. If the angle on the inside (interior) of the polygon (think the inside angle of a triangle) is 45°, the exterior angle would be 135°. The two angles, both interior and exterior, will add up to 180°.

F – Face through Fundamental Theorem of Arithmetic

Face – The face is the flat surface of a solid object (three-dimensional shape); that flat surface of a polyhedron. A die a six faces.

Factor – A factor is a whole number that divides into another number evenly. It is a number that is multiplied together with another number to get another number (called the product). 5 x 4 = 20. The 5 and 4 are factors of 20 (20 is the product). The complete list of factors for 20 is 1, 2, 4, 5, 10, and 20.

Factor Tree – A factor tree is a diagram that can be used to detect prime factors of a composite number. It's writing a number as a product of its prime factors. 36 = "2" x 18; 18 = "2" x 9; 9 = "3" x "3". The number 36 as a product of its prime factors is 2 x 2 x 3 x 3 = 36.

Factorial – Factorial is the outcome of multiplying a whole number by every whole number down to one. The factorial symbol is the exclamation point "!". Four factorial, written 4!, equals 4 x 3 x 2 x 1. The answer is 24. 15! = 15 x 14 x 13... x 1 = 1,307,674,368,000.

Factoring – Factoring is discovering what needs to be multiplied to get a mathematical expression. 4x - 20 = 4(x - 5). The factors of this expression are 4 and (x – 5).

Fahrenheit (°F) - Fahrenheit is a scale that measures temperature. Water freezes at 32° F (0° C). Water boils at 212° F (100° C). A normal human body temperature is 98.6° F.

Feet – Feet is the plural of foot, which is 12 inches. The lake is 15 feet at the center.

Few – A few is more than two (which is a couple) but less than many.

Fibonacci Sequence – Named after the Italian mathematician, Leonardo Fibonacci (1175-1250), in the Fibonacci Sequence, each number equals the sum (addition) of the two numbers before it. 0, 1, 1, 2, 3, 5, 8, 13, 21, 34, 55, 89, 144...

Finite Number – A finite number is a number that can be counted (or measured) and has an end, versus an infinite number that does not have an end. The number of seashells in the ocean is finite. Counting by 2's has no end…it will go on forever, and is therefore, infinite.

First – First is the very beginning; number one. She won the race by finishing in first place. After hitting the ball he ran to first base.

Flashcards – Flashcards contain problems to help with practice or mastery of a subject area. $5x + 6 = 46$ might be on the front of the card to solve for x. The answer, $x = 8$, would be on the back of the flashcard to check for accuracy.

Flat – A flat is a block of 100. Math manipulative blocks that show base 10 numbers values. One (1) three-dimensional block is called a "short." Ten (10) three-dimensional blocks stacked on top of one another is called a "long." One hundred (100) three-dimensional blocks stacked ten high and ten wide, 10 x 10, is called a "flat." One thousand (1,000) three-dimensional blocks stacked ten high, ten wide, and ten deep (looks like a cube), 10 x 10 x 10, is called a "block."

Flip – Flipping (turning) an object will create a mirror image of itself. Also, when dividing fractions, the sign is changed from division to multiplication and the second number has to flip (also called taking the reciprocal) in order to be able to solve this type of math problem.

Fluid Ounce (fl. oz.) – A fluid ounce is a measurement of volume. One cup is equivalent to 8 fluid ounces.

FOIL (Method) – The FOIL method is an acronym that means First, Outside, Inside, and Last. This method is used when multiplying two binomials together by use of the distributive property. To solve $(x - 5)(x + 4)$ results in the following: Multiply the "First," x times $x = x^2$. Next, multiply the "Outside," x times $4 = 4x$. Now, multiply the "Inside," -5 times $x = -5x$. Finally, multiply the "Last," -5 times $4 = -20$. We now have $x^2 + 4x - 5x - 20$. Simplifying gives our final answer of $x^2 - x - 20$.

Foot (ft.) – A foot is a unit of measurement that measures length. One foot equals 12 inches. Three feet equal a yard. One mile contains 5,280 feet.

Formula – A series of numbers and symbols that express how to work out a problem. To figure out the area of a room the following formula is used: area = length x width. To figure out the area of a circle the following formula is used: area = π x r² (pi times the radius squared).

Fortnight – Fortnight is a period of 14 days.

Fraction – A fraction is part of a whole (group or number). A fraction is also a number divided by another number. A fraction has both a numerator (top number) and a denominator (bottom number). 1/2, 3/4, 5/8, and 15/16 are all called proper fractions. 5/2, 8/3, 15/14, and 7/1 are all called improper fractions. These improper fractions would be simplified (reduced to lowest terms) into what are called mixed numbers (numerals). They would be simplified as follows: 2-1/2, 2-2/3, 1-1/14, and 7 respectively.

Fraction Bar – A fraction bar is the bar or line (—, /) that separates the numerator and denominator.

Frequency – The frequency is how often something happens (during a period of time) or appears (data set). The engine spins at 2,500 rpm's (rounds per minute). The frequency is 2,500. That's how many times the engine spun over a period of 1 minute. With a data set of 50 test scores, the number grade 88 appeared 13 times. The frequency is 13. That's how many times the test score of 88 appeared on the data set of 50 test scores.

Frequency Distribution Table – A frequency distribution table is generally used in statistics. It is used to document and record data. The phone rang 30 times during the week. On Monday, the phone rang 4 times, Tuesday, 3 times, Wednesday, and Thursday, not at all; on Friday, the phone rang 6 times, Saturday, 7 times, and Sunday, 10 times. The frequency distribution table would have the days labeled Monday through Sunday and the frequency (the number of times the phone rang) next to the corresponding day.

Frequency Histogram – A frequency histogram is a graph that uses vertical columns to illustrate the number of times (frequency) an event happens. A class of 4th grade students (24 students) was asked how many hours of sleep they get each night. The results were as follows: 4 students get 7-8 hours, 8 students get 8-9 hours, 9 students get 9-10 hours, and 3 students get 10-11 hours. This data would get recorded on a frequency histogram.

Frequency Polygon – A frequency polygon is a graph made from using a frequency histogram where the top points of each column (in the middle) are joined together, forming a polygon. This gives the appearance (a visual) of the rises and the falls of the data.

Frustum – The frustum is the result (the piece that is left) of a solid cone or pyramid once the top of it is sliced or removed (cut off).

Function – A function is a mathematical relationship between two values. Every input will result in one output. A function often looks like this: f(x). A value (input) is put in for x and the result is the output. For the problem 4 + x, if the input for x is 1, the output is 5. If the input for x is 7, the output is 11. If the input for x is -2, the output is 2.

Fundamental Theorem of Arithmetic – Every whole number, other than one (one is not a prime number), can be written as a product of prime numbers (prime number factors are one and itself), also called prime factorization. Each number according to the fundamental theorem of arithmetic has unique prime number decomposition. The first ten prime numbers are: 2, 3, 5, 7, 11, 13, 17, 19, 23, and 29. Listed are three numbers that are written as products of prime numbers per the fundamental theorem of arithmetic: 25, 75, and 88; 25 = 5 x 5; 75 = 3 x 5 x 5; 88 = 2 x 2 x 2 x 11.

G – Gallon through Grouping

Gallon (gal) – A gallon is a unit of measurement for measuring liquids (volume). One gallon equals 4 quarts, 8 pints, and 128 fluid ounces.

Geo Board – A geo board is used to make shapes and patterns. The shapes and patterns are made on a pegged-board with elastic bands (rubber bands can also be used).

Geo Strips – Geo strips are used to make geometric shapes, such as squares, triangles, etc.

Geometry – Geometry is a part of mathematics that deals with points, lines (including segments and rays), angles (including acute, obtuse, and right), and curves (circles), and the relationship they have regarding space. Geometry also deals with surface areas (triangles, squares, pentagons, etc.) and solid objects (cubes, spheres, cones, pyramids, etc.)

Gigaliter (GL) – A gigaliter is a unit of measurement that measures huge quantities of liquid. A gigaliter is equal to 1 billion liters. Giga is a prefix that means billion.

Googol – A googol is 10^{100}. A googol is a 1 followed by 100 zeros; hence, 10,000,000,000,000,000,000,000,000,000,000,000,000,000,000,000,000,000,000,000,000,000,000,000,000,000,000,000,000,000,000,000,000,000.

Gradient – The gradient is simply the measurement of the steepness of a straight line as defined by the equation of a straight line. Equation of a straight line consists of plugging in data to see if it satisfies the equation. On the coordinate plane, the coordinates are (-3, -1). Does this satisfy the equation $y = x + 2$? Plugging in the numbers results in -1 = -3 + 2. Simplifying this statement results in -1 = -1. This equation is satisfied.

Gram (g) – A gram is a unit of measurement that measures weight. 1,000 grams is equivalent to 1 kilogram. Kilo is a prefix that means 1,000.

Graph – A graph is a diagram or drawing that is used to keep a record of information and illustrate values. A graph is also used as a visual to help better understand data rather than displaying a bunch of numbers. Types of graphs that are commonly used today are line graphs, pie charts, bar charts, and area graphs, and others.

Greater Than – Greater than means bigger, greater, and more than, etc. The symbol (>) is often referred to an alligator's mouth. $8 > 5$; $5 \times 4 > 5 + 4$; $5^2 > 2^3 + 15$

Greatest Common Factor (GCF) – The greatest common factor is the largest number that evenly divides (goes into) two or more numbers. For the numbers 8, 12, 20, and 100, the greatest common factor is 4. For the numbers 10, 13, and 21, the greatest common factor is 1. For the numbers 36 and 45, the greatest common factor is 9.

Grid Paper – Grid paper, or graph paper, is paper ruled into small equal squares (also ruled into triangles or dots) to allow the drawing of graphs, charts, and diagrams.

Gross – One gross is equal to 12 dozen (144 total). Gross is the total of everything. Gross mass would include the weight of the element and the flask (the net weight would include the weight of only the element). Gross pay would include all money earned before taxes and any other deductions, such as health insurance or child support (net pay, sometimes referred to as take-home pay, would include the money left over after all taxes and deductions are removed from the gross pay).

Grouping – Grouping is to divide stuff into equal sets, or groups. If there are 24 players and 6 players are needed for each team, 4 groups, or teams, could be formed.

H – Half through Hypotenuse

Half – A half is splitting a whole of something into two equal parts. You and I will share this apple pie equally. We will both eat half. We'll split this $20.00, 50-50, and each of us will get $10.00.

Hand Span – A hand span is taking the outstretched hand and measuring the distance fully across between the tip of the thumb to the tip of the little finger.

Hect – Hect is a prefix that means 100.

Hectare (ha) – A hectare is a standard unit of measurement in the metric system that measures large areas (similar to the acre). One hectare is equal to 10,000 square meters. One hectare (ha) is equivalent to approximately 2.47 acres.

Hectometer (hm) – One hectometer is equivalent to 100 meters. One hectometer is approximately 109 yards, or slightly more than a football field.

Heft (Hefting) – To heft is to hold or lift something in your hand to test (estimate) the weight of it.

Height – The height is the vertical measurement of something from top to bottom. The height of my dog is 42". The tree in my back yard is approximately 12' (from the ground to the top branch).

Hemisphere – A hemisphere is half of a sphere (geometric shape). The Earth has two hemispheres: the Northern Hemisphere and the Southern Hemisphere. The equator (imaginary line around the Earth) splits the Earth (sphere) in half.

Hendecagon – A hendecagon (flat-shaped polygon) has 11 straight sides. This polygon is also known as an undecagon.

Hepta – Hepta is a prefix for the number 7.

Heptagon - A heptagon (flat-shaped polygon) has 7 straight sides. It is also called a septagon.

Hexa – Hexa is a prefix for the number 6.

Hexadecimal – A hexadecimal is a base-sixteen number system that is usually associated with computers. It is a unique way to set up color (colors). The hexadecimal symbols are: 0, 1, 2, 3, 4, 5, 6, 7, 8, and 9, A, B, C, D, E, and F.

Hexagon - A hexagon (flat-shaped polygon) has 6 straight sides.

Hexahedron – A hexahedron is a cube (polyhedron) with 6 sides, or faces (Think of a six-sided die).

Highest Common Factor (HCF) - The highest (greatest) common factor is the largest number that evenly divides (goes into) two or more numbers. For the numbers 4, 16, 24, and 48, the greatest common factor is 4. For the numbers 8, 11, and 19, the greatest common factor is 1. For the numbers 16 and 48, the greatest common factor is 16.

Hindu-Arabic Number System – The Hindu-Arabic Number System is the number system that is used today. It contains the numbers (digits) 1, 2, 3, 4, 5, 6, 7, 8, 9, and 0.

Histogram - A histogram is a bar graph that uses vertical columns to represent frequency distribution for certain ranges (of data) or intervals (the number of times (the frequency) an event happens). Three classes of 12th grade students (74 students) were asked how many hours they study each week. The results were as follows: 6 students study less than 3 hours per week, 33 students study 3-6 hours per week, 27 students study 6-10 hours per week, and 8 students study more than 10 hours per week. This data would get recorded on a histogram.

Horizontal – Something horizontal is parallel (goes side to side, left to right) to the horizon. The x-axis on the coordinate plane is horizontal.

Hour – An hour is a unit (period) of time that equals 60 minutes. One day is 24 hours.

Hour Hand – The hour hand is the smallest hand on an analog clock that represents the hour of the day. It takes 12 hours to circle the clock once, and two round-trips to equal one full day.

Hundred – A hundred (100) is a whole number. It is the first three-digit number. 10 x 10 = 100. One hundred (100) three-dimensional base-ten blocks stacked ten high and ten wide, 10 x 10, is called a "flat.

Hundredth – A hundredth is 1/100 of something. One hundredth is taking something and dividing it into 100 equal parts. One penny (cent) is one hundredth of a dollar.

Hyperbola – A hyperbola (one of the conic sections) looks like an arch; it is curve-shaped.

Hypotenuse – The hypotenuse is the opposite side (the longest side, the sloped side) of the right angle in a right triangle. In reference to the Pythagorean Theorem, $a^2 + b^2 = c^2$, the "c^2" is the hypotenuse.

I – Icosahedron through Iterative

Icosahedron – An icosahedron is a polyhedron (flat-sided three-dimensional solid object) that has 20 faces. Think of a 20-sided die with each of the 20 sides (faces) looking like congruent equilateral triangles. An icosahedron is one of the platonic solids.

Identity Property for Addition – The Identity Property for Addition, also known as the Identity Property of zero, states that a number won't change if zero is added to the number. The number + zero = the same (identical) number. $8 + 0 = 8$; $3y + 0 = 3y$; $r + 0 = r$

Identity Property for Multiplication - The Identity Property for Multiplication, also known as the Identity Property of one, states that a number won't change if one is multiplied to the number. The number x one = the same (identical) number. $8 \times 1 = 8$; $3y \times 1 = 3y$; $r \times 1 = r$

Imaginary Number – An imaginary number is a complex number of the form a + bi, where b is nonzero. $i = \sqrt{-1}$ or $i^2 = -1$.

Impossible – In probability, the chance, or outcome of an event with a probability of 0 has no chance, or it's impossible for the event, or outcome, to happen.

Improper Fraction - An improper fraction is when the numerator (top number) is larger, or greater, than the denominator (bottom number). When simplifying an improper fraction, the final answer becomes a mixed number. Examples of improper fractions are as follows: 7/3, 8/1, 10/9, 16/5, 17/8, 7/4. Simplifying these types of fractions will be explained in the chapter Reducing Improper Fractions to Simplest Form, Creating a Mixed Number. The above fractions reduced to simplest form would equal 2-1/3, 8, 1-1/9, 3-1/5, 2-1/8, and 1-3/4.

Inch (in.) - An inch is a unit of measurement that measures length. Twelve inches equals 1 foot. Thirty-six inches measures 1 yard. There are 2.54 centimeters in every inch.

Incircle – The incircle is the circle inside of a polygon where the circumference of this circle touches the middle (midpoint) of each side of the polygon. The incircle's radius is called the apothem.

Increase - Increase means to make bigger, to make greater, or to get larger when referring to a number or to the size of an object.

Independent Events - An independent event is an outcome (or occurrence) that is not affected by prior outcomes and does not affect the probability of the event. If you want to roll a 5 on a die, there is a 1 in 6 chance of that happening. On the second roll, there is still a 1 in 6 chance of that happening, and so forth. The previous rolls will not affect the outcome of the next roll, or any other rolls after that.

Index (Power of, Exponent, Raised) – The index dictates the number of times the base is multiplied by itself. The base is the number that is multiplied by itself by the number of times, as determined by the exponent (index). Five (the "base") to the third power (the "index"), written 5^3, would be expressed 5 x 5 x 5 = 125.

Inequality – Inequality states that two numbers or values are not equal ($\neq$).

Infinite – An infinite number is a number that does not have an end, versus a finite number that can be counted (or measured) and does have an end. Counting by 1's has no end...it will go on forever, and is therefore, infinite. The number of blades of grass on a football field can be counted (but who would want to?) and is a finite number.

Infinity (∞) – Infinity...cannot be counted... it goes on...forever...it never ends...

Integer – Integers include all the negative numbers, all the positive numbers, and zero. Fractions and decimals are not integers. -50, -33, -1, 0, 1, 16, 125, and 1,000,000 are all examples of integers.

Intercept - The coordinate plane is the plane that contains both the x-axis and the y-axis. These two axes are perpendicular to each other and intersect at the point of origin, or (0, 0). The x-intercept of a line is the point at which the line crosses the x-axis (the y value equals 0). The y-intercept of a line is the point at which the line crosses the y-axis (the x value equals 0).

Interest – Interest is money that is either paid or earned for using someone else's money. I have a home mortgage loan that I am paying 5.50% interest on the balance owed. I invested my money in stocks that earned 9.75% over the past two years. The formula for interest is: Interest = Principal x Rate x Time

Interest Rate – The interest rate is the amount, usually in percentage form, one has to pay back for borrowing money. The interest rate on my credit card is 12.99%. If I carry a balance of $5,000 for one year, the amount of interest I will have to pay back (on top of the $5,000) is $649.50.

Interior Angle – An interior angle is an angle that is inside a polygon. An equilateral triangle has three interior angles of 60° each. A square has four interior angles (right angles) of 90° each. Also, two parallel lines intersected by a transversal line has four interior angles (the angles may vary in size).

Intersect/Intersection – To intersect is to cross over at a common point.

Interval – An interval can be the amount of time between two events and it can also be the distance between two points.

Inverse – Inverse is taking the opposite or reversing operations. The inverse of addition is subtraction. The inverse of multiplication is division. The inverse of squaring a number is taking the root of the number. 5 + 9 = 14, the inverse is 14 – 9 = 5; 8 x 4 = 32, the inverse is 32 ÷ 4 = 8; 6^2 (6 x 6) = 36, the inverse is $\sqrt{36}$ = 6

Irrational Number – An irrational number is any number that is not rational. An irrational number is not a fraction (5/2), it doesn't terminate (2.589), and it doesn't repeat (3.33333…). The best example of an irrational number is pi (π). It's not a fraction, it doesn't terminate (it goes on forever) and there is no repeated pattern. Pi is 3.14159265… (Do a web search for "1 million digits of pi")

Irregular – An irregular shape (polygon) has one or more unequal sides and one or more unequal angles. An equilateral triangle and a square are regular polygons. An isosceles triangle and a rectangle are irregular polygons.

Isometric – Something isometric has equal dimensions or measurements. An 8" x 8" sheet of graph paper is isometric.

Isosceles Triangle – An isosceles triangle has two sides that are equal (congruent), in addition to two angles that are equal (congruent).

Iterative – Something that is iterative is repeating.

J – Jump Strategy

Jump Strategy – The jump strategy helps to work out a calculation by jumping parts of a number (a number line can be created), usually by tens and ones. 27 + 31, start the number line at 27. Then add 10 + 10 + 10 + 1. This equals 58.

K – Kilo through Km/h

Kilo – The prefix kilo stands for one thousand.

Kilogram (kg) – The kilogram (metric) is the standard unit to measure weight. One kilogram is equal to 1,000 grams. The weight of 1 kilogram is a little more than 2.2 pounds.

Kiloliter (kl) - The kiloliter (metric) is the standard unit to measure liquid. One kiloliter is equal to 1,000 liters. The volume of 1 kiloliter is a little more than 264 gallons.

Kilometer (km) - The kilometer (metric) is the standard unit to measure distance. One kilometer is equal to 1,000 meters. The length of 1 kilometer is a little more than 1,093 yards, or almost 11 football fields.

Kite – A kite (plane-shaped quadrilateral) has two pairs of equal sides that are adjacent, and one set of equal, opposite angles.

Km/h – km/h (metric) is the standard unit to measure speed. It is the abbreviation for kilometers per hour. 100 kilometers per hour is approximately 62 miles per hour.

L – Lateral Surface Area through Lowest Terms

Lateral Surface Area – The lateral surface area of a three-dimensional object is the total area (area = length x width) of the surface. The base, or bases, of the object are not included. A six-sided die's surface area (assume the die is on a table) would be the combined area of the four sides. The top and bottom areas on the die would not be included.

Leap Year – A leap year occurs every four years. There was one this year on February 29, 2012, and the next one will be on February 29, 2016. The reason we have leap year is due to Earth's revolution around the sun. It takes the Earth 365 1/4 days to make one complete revolution around the sun (one year). We can't make up 1/4 of a day. After four years (four quarters make a whole) we add a 366th day to the calendar (February 29), whereas the other three years have 365 calendar days.

Lease – A lease, most commonly used for renting homes and cars, is a legal contract that explains the terms and conditions (amount, term length, etc.) of the asset that you are using (borrowing).

Least – The least is the smallest of the population (use least when comparing three or more things). Of the numbers 2, 1.75, 3/4, and .6, the smallest, or least of these is .6. Between a gallon, a pint, and a quart, a pint holds the least amount of liquid.

Least Common Denominator (LCD) – In fractions, the least common denominator is the smallest number (lowest common multiple) the denominators (bottom number) will divide into evenly, without any remainders. For the fractions 1/2 and 11/12, the least common denominator is 12. Both the 2 and the 12 go into 12 evenly (Note: the least common denominator can never be smaller than the largest denominator). For the fractions 5/6 and 3/8, the least common denominator is 24. Both the 6 and the 8 go into 24 evenly. There is no number smaller than 24 that both 6 and 8 go into evenly. Therefore, 24 is the least common denominator.

Least Common Multiple (LCM) – The least common multiple is the smallest number that is a multiple of two or more numbers. The least common multiple of 2, 4, 6, and 8 is 24 (Trick: take the largest of the numbers and see if the other numbers go into that number. If not, then take the next multiple of the largest number, and so on). The least common multiple of 5, 6, and 10 is 30.

Length – The length of something is its distance from end to end. It tells how long something is, depending on the unit of measurement. Length can be determined in millimeters (mm), centimeters (cm), inches (in.), feet (ft.), yards (yd.), meters (m), kilometers (km), miles (mi.), and more. The length of a football field is 300 feet, or 100 yards. My pencil is 15 centimeters (cm) in length.

Less – Less is fewer, not as many (use less when comparing 2 things). You have $20. I have $17. I have less money than you.

Less Than - Less than means something is smaller than something else. The symbol (<) is often referred to an alligator's mouth. $8 < 10$; $3 \times 2 < 5 + 2$; $3^2 < 2^3 + 3$

Like Fractions – Like fractions are fractions that have the same denominator. 5/12 and 1/12 are like fractions.

Like Terms – Terms (a number, variable, or the product of a number and a variable(s)) are considered "like" when their numbers and variables (in additions to any exponents) are similar, or the same. $3x^2$ and $2x^2$ are like terms. a^2y^3 and $9a^2y^3$ are like terms. $5x^2$ and $2x$ are not like terms. $7x$ and $2y$ are not like terms.

Likelihood – A probability term, likelihood is the chance that a specific event or outcome will happen. What is the likelihood that if I flip a coin 2 times, 2 heads will appear in a row? The answer, or the probability, or the likelihood that would happen is there would be a 25% chance of 2 heads appearing in a row. $1/2 \times 1/2 = 1/4 = 25\%$

Likely - In mathematical probability, the likelihood of an outcome, or desired result, is measured on a scale, ranging from 0 to 1. If the conclusion is 0, the event, or outcome, is impossible; there is a 0% chance of it happening. If the conclusion is 1, the outcome is said to be "certain" to happen; there is a 100% chance that it will happen. If there is a 75% chance of an event, or occurrence, happening, the outcome is said to be "likely," or even probable that it will happen.

Limit – The limit is the edge, point, or line beyond which something may not or cannot proceed.

Line – A line is straight, extending in both directions, and has no beginning or end (If there is a beginning or an end it is not a line anymore. It would then be a ray or a line segment).

Line Graph (Chart) – A line graph is a graph that shows how something has changed in value. This graph uses plotted points (that represent the data), and these points are connected by lines.

Line of Best Fit – The line of best fit is a straight line drawn on a scatter plot (graph) to show the general direction that a group of points seem to be heading to present a clearer view of the data.

Line of Reflection – The line of reflection is a line that is midway between an object and its mirrored reflection. The original object has an image that is the same distance from the line of reflection, as is its reflection. The original point is on the opposite side of the line. This reflection is flipped and the size does not change.

Line Plot – Like a dot plot, a line plot uses a number line that represents a population (sample). One dot is used (and is placed on the corresponding number) for each member of the sample. The dots are stacked up if more than one dot represents the same number. If test scores are 80, 81, 85, 86, 86, and 89, a dot (line) plot could range from 80 to 90. Each score would have one dot on it except for the score of 86. It would consist of two dots.

Line Segment – A line segment is a piece, or section, of a line. The line segment is defined because endpoints are on both ends of the segment.

Line Symmetry – Line (or reflection) symmetry is an imaginary line whereby folding the image would have both halves being an exact match; one half is the reflection of the other half.

Linear – Usually referring to a line, something linear goes in a straight direction. Being linear is being one-dimensional.

Linear Equation – A linear equation, when graphed, marks a straight line. The general equation is $y = mx + b$, where y (how high) = m (slope –

change in y / change in x) times x (how far) + b (the Y Intercept – where the line crosses the y-axis)

Linear Scale – A linear scale has equal divisions that are evenly spaced; a scale, a ruler, a thermometer, etc. Each of the intervals, pounds, inches, and degrees are the same and are considered linear.

Lines (Types) - A line is straight, extending in both directions, and has no beginning or end. There are many types of lines and include, but are not limited to, the following: concurrent (two or more intersecting lines at a single point), converging (heading toward a single point), curved (not straight), diagonal (join non-adjacent corners of a polygon), horizontal (parallel to the horizon), intersecting (crossing over each other), oblique (angled to the horizon), parallel (the exact same distance apart), perpendicular (90° right angles to each other), and vertical (90° right angles to the horizon).

Liquidity – Liquidity, or liquidating as it is most commonly used, is taking all of one's assets (houses, cars, and anything of value) and converting them to cash.

Liter (L) - The liter (metric) is the standard unit to measure liquid, or capacity. Four liters is equal to 1.06 US gallons.

Locus – The locus is a set or configuration of all points (coordinates) whose location satisfies or shares a property, or is determined by one or more specified conditions (equations or algebraic) that usually results in a curve.

Logarithm – The logarithm of a number is the exponent by which another fixed value, the base, has to be raised to produce that number. For example, the logarithm of 64 to base 4 is 3, because 64 is 4 to the third power; $64 = 4^3 = 4 \times 4 \times 4$. The formula is $\log_b(x)$; $\log_4(64) = 3$.

Logic – Logic is the science that deals with the principles of reasoning, and constructing propositions as distinguished from their content and of method and validity in regards to deductive reasoning.

Long - A long is a block of 10. Math manipulative blocks that show base 10 numbers values. One (1) three-dimensional block is called a "short." Ten (10) three-dimensional blocks stacked on top of one another is called a "long." One hundred (100) three-dimensional blocks stacked ten high and ten wide, 10 x 10, is called a "flat." One thousand (1,000) three-dimensional blocks stacked ten high, ten wide, and ten deep (looks like a cube), 10 x 10 x 10, is called a "block."

Long Division – Long division is a method for solving division problems. It is a unique process that assists in answering division problems that, once mastered, allows for the problems to be quickly solved.

Lowest Common Denominator (LCD) – Identical to that of the least common denominator, the lowest common denominator, in fractions, is the smallest number (lowest common multiple) the denominators (bottom number) will divide into evenly, without any remainders. For the fractions 1/2 and 11/12, the lowest common denominator is 12. Both the 2 and the 12 go into 12 evenly (Note: the lowest common denominator can never be smaller than the largest denominator). For the fractions 5/6 and 3/8, the lowest common denominator is 24. Both the 6 and the 8 go into 24 evenly. There is no number smaller than 24 that both 6 and 8 go into evenly. Therefore, 24 is the lowest common denominator.

Lowest Terms – Also known as reducing and simplifying fractions, a fraction is reduced to lowest terms when both the numerator (top number) and the denominator (bottom number) have no common factors other than one. For the fraction 8/12, there is a common number (factor) other than one that goes into both numbers evenly. Four goes into both numbers. Dividing both the numerator and denominator by 4 simplifies this fraction to 2/3. This fraction is now in its lowest terms.

M – MAB Blocks through Mutually Exclusive Events

MAB Blocks – Like base ten blocks, MAB blocks are math manipulative blocks that show base 10 number values. One (1) three-dimensional block is called a "short." Ten (10) three-dimensional blocks stacked on top of one another is called a "long." One hundred (100) three-dimensional blocks stacked ten high and ten wide, 10 x 10, is called a "flat." One thousand (1,000) three-dimensional blocks stacked ten high, ten wide, and ten deep (looks like a cube), 10 x 10 x 10, is called a "block."

Magic Square – A magic square (logic puzzle) is a square grid (3 x 3, 4 x 4, etc.) filled with arranged numbers so that the total of each row, column, and diagonal is the same. It's along the same idea as the popular game Sudoku.

Major Arc – The major arc of a circle is the larger of the two arcs of the circumference of the circle, when it is divided into two arcs (the smaller one is called the minor arc). Think of a round, delicious chocolate cake that just came out of the oven. Cut yourself a slice and eat it. The slice you just ate (unless you ate the bigger piece) would be the minor arc. The remaining cake is the major arc.

Map – A map (paper or digital, GPS) is a tool used to help find and locate places. It displays cities, landmarks, rivers, and roads to guide travelers to their destinations.

Mass – Mass (also see density) is the amount of matter in an object. A 2" x 3" x 6" piece of wood has more mass than a 2" x 3" x 6" piece of Styrofoam. A 1" diameter 18" long lead pipe has more mass than a 1" diameter 18" long solid iron pipe. The lead pipe contains more mass, and therefore, has more matter than the iron pipe (note: weight pertains to gravity, not mass).

Mathematics – Using processes (operations), symbols, and varying rules, Mathematics studies numbers, shapes, patterns, space, quantities, and so much more. Some of the branches of Mathematics include, but are not limited to: Algebra, Analysis, Arithmetic, Calculus, Differential Equations, Geometry, Number Theory, Probability & Statistics, and Topology.

Matrix – A matrix is a set of quantities in a rectangular array.

Maximum – The maximum (number, value, amount, etc.) is the largest or the greatest. What is the maximum number to make the statement true? Of the set {3, 5, 7, 8, and 10}, x + 5 < 14; the maximum number is 8.

Mean – The mean is the average of something. For the first five basketball games, Larry scored 27, 22, 31, 17, and 35 points respectively. What is the mean? To figure out the mean, or average, two calculations are made. First, all the numbers in the data set are added together. Second, the total sum is then divided by the number of elements in the data set. Adding the five scores results in 132 points scored. Taking 132 and dividing it by 5 (5 games played) results in 26.4 points per game. Larry's mean score (average) is 26.4 points per game.

Measure – To measure is to find a total (some standard unit) that shows the amount, or size, of something.

Measurement - (also see measure) some standard units of measurement are as follows: Area (acres, square units), Currency (US dollar, Euro), Distance (centimeters, inches, feet, yards, miles, kilometers, light years), Power (calories, BTU, horsepower, watts, joules), Pressure (microbar, psi, pascal), Speed (angstrom, furlongs, microns), Temperature (Celsius, Fahrenheit, Kelvin), Time (nanoseconds, seconds, minutes, hours, days, weeks, months, years, decades, centuries), Volume (barrels, cubic feet, cubic yards, gallons, liters, pints, quarts, tablespoons, teaspoons), and Weight (grams, kilograms, ounces, pounds, tons),

Median – The median is the "middle" number in a data set when listed in either ascending or descending order. It means that half of the numbers are below the median and half of the numbers are above the median. Sometimes the median is a better representation of a data set rather than taking the mean because the mean may be skewed with outlying circumstances, such as a few figures being extremely lower or extremely higher that would greatly affect the mean. To get the median for an "odd" number data set, just take the middle number. For the numbers 25, 30, 40, 72, 73, 75, and 100, the median number is 72 (the average "mean" is 59.3). To get the median for an "even" number data set, take the two middle numbers and average them. For the numbers 25, 30, 40, 72, 73, 75, the median number is 56 (40 + 72 / 2); (the average "mean" is 52.5).

Megaliter (ML) - The megaliter is the standard metric unit to measure large amounts of liquid. One megaliter is equal to 1,000,000 liters. The volume of 1 megaliter is a little more than 264,172 gallons. An Olympic sized pool holds a little more than 660,430 gallons. 2.5 megaliters will fill an Olympic sized pool.

Member – A member is an element of a set. The letter M is a member of the set {M, A, T, H}.

Meter (m) - The meter (metric) is the standard unit to measure length (or distance). One meter is equal to 100 centimeters. The length of 1 meter is 39.37 inches, or 1.09 yards.

Metric System – The Metric System uses multiples of ten for their decimal system of measurement. 100 centimeters equals 1 meter. 1,000 meters equals 1 kilometer. 1,000 milliliters equals 1 liter. 1,000 grams equals 1 kilogram. 1,000 kilograms equals 1 ton (metric). Water freezes at 0° Celsius and boils at 100° Celsius.

Midday – Midday is halfway through the day, or 12:00 PM (noon).

Midnight - Midnight is halfway through the night, or 12:00 AM (00:00 military time).

Midpoint – The midpoint is halfway (the middle) through something. The midpoint divides a line segment in half. The midpoint of our 25 mile trip is 12.5 miles.

Mile (mi) – A mile is the standard unit to measure distance. One mile is equal to 5,280 feet. The distance from New York to Los Angeles, California is approximately 2,800 miles.

Millennium – a millennium is a time period of 1,000 years.

Milli – Milli, a prefix, is $1/1,000^{th}$ of something. One thousandth is taking something and dividing it into 1,000 equal parts. One meter consists of 1,000 millimeters. One liter contains 1,000 milliliters.

Milliliter (mL) - The milliliter (metric) is the standard unit to measure (small amounts) capacity, or volume. One milliliter is equal to $1/1,000^{th}$ of a liter. One gallon contains approximately 3,785 milliliters.

Millimeter (mm) - The millimeter (metric) is the standard unit to measure (small) length. One millimeter is equal to 1/1,000th of a meter. One foot is approximately 305 millimeters.

Million - A million contains a one, followed by six (6) zeros. A million (1,000,000) is a thousand thousands.

Minimum - The minimum (number, value, amount, etc.) is the smallest or the least. What is the minimum number to make the statement true? Of the set {2, 5, 6, 9, and 11}, x - 5 > 2; the minimum number is 9.

Minor Arc - The minor arc of a circle is the smaller of the two arcs of the circumference of the circle, when it is divided into two arcs (the larger one is called the major arc). Think of a round, hot apple pie that just came out of the oven. Cut yourself one small slice and eat it. The slice you just ate is the minor arc. The remaining pie is the major arc.

Minuend – Used when performing a subtraction problem, the minuend is the digit that is subtracted "from." For the problem 20 – 3 = 17, the minuend is the 20. (Note: the 17 is the difference and the 3 is called the subtrahend)

Minus – To minus is to subtract, decrease by, take-away, or take the difference of. 15 minus 12 equals 3

Minute - A minute is a unit (period) of time that equals 60 seconds. One hour equals 60 minutes. One day equals 1,440 minutes.

Minute Hand - The minute hand is the larger of the two hands on an analog clock that represents the minutes of the hour. It takes 60 minutes for the minute hand to circle the clock once, and 24 round-trips to equal one full day.

Mirror Image – A mirror image is an identical reflection of an object (person), only reversed (the left side would be on the right, and visa-versa).

Mixed Number (Fraction) - A mixed number (or mixed fraction) contains a whole number and a fraction. The fraction in a mixed number always needs to be checked to see if it can be reduced, or simplified further. The mixed number 2-3/4 is pronounced two (2) whole and three (3) over four

(4) or, two and three-fourths. The 2 is the whole number, the 3 is the numerator, and the 4 is the denominator.

Mode – Usually used in relation with the "mean" and the "median," the mode is the number (or piece of data) that appears most frequently in a data set. For the set {1, 2, 3, 3, 4, 5, 6, 7, 8, 8, 8, 9, 10}, the mode is 8. For the set {1, 2, 3, 4, 5}, there is no mode.

Monomial - A monomial is a polynomial that has one term, $6x$, $2x^2y^3$; x^2, 16; $2xy$

Month – Twelve months make up a full year. The months add up to 365 days and 366 days every fourth year (February 29), which is leap year. January has 31 days. February has 28 days (except every fourth year it has 29). March has 31 days. April has 30 days. May has 31 days. June has 30 days. July has 31 days. August has 31 days. September has 30 days. October has 31 days. November has 30 days. December has 31 days.

More - More is larger (use more when comparing 2 things). You read 10 books and I read 8 books. You read more books than I.

Most - The most is the largest of the population (use most when comparing three or more things). Of the monetary values $3.05, $1.95, $2.60, and $2, $3.05 has the most value; between a foot, a meter, and a yard, a meter has the most length (or distance).

MPG (Miles Per Gallon) – The distance (miles) something gets (a motorcycle, car, truck, etc.) per one gallon of fuel consumption (usually gasoline). My car went 410 miles on a tank of gas (I refueled using 10.85 gallons of gas). $410 \div 10.85 = 37.8$ MPG.

MPH (Miles Per Hour) – The distance (miles) something travels in one hour. I walked 5 miles in 2 hours ($5 \div 2$). I averaged 2.5 miles per hour. I traveled from Pennsylvania to Orlando (1080 miles) in 18.5 hours ($1080 \div 18.5$). I averaged 58.4 miles per hour. You are going 70 miles per hour. This means that if you travel at that speed continuously for one hour you will have traveled 70 miles.

Multiple – A multiple is the outcome when multiplying, or when adding a number to itself a specific number of times (multiplication is repeated addition). 8 x 6 = 48. 48 is a multiple of both 6 and 8; 8 + 8 + 8 + 8 + 8 + 8 = 48

Multiplicand – The multiplicand (also known as a factor) is the number that is being multiplied. 5 x 11 = 55. The 11 is the multiplicand.

Multiplication – Multiplication, a mathematical operation, is repeated addition. 3 x 4 = 12, or 3 + 3 + 3 + 3 = 12; 2.5 x 5 = 12.5, or 2.5 + 2.5 + 2.5 + 2.5 + 2.5 = 12.5

Multiplication Principle – The multiplication principle is a strategy used to figure out outcomes, or possibilities (probability). I have 6 different pairs of pants, 10 different colored dress shirts, 5 different ties, and 3 different pairs of shoes. How many different ways (combinations) can be made without repeating the same outfit? Using the multiplication principle, 6 (pants) x 10 (shirts) x 5 (ties) x 3 (shoes), or 6 x 10 x 5 x 3 = 900.

Multiplication Table – A multiplication table is a tool used to help find a result when multiplying two numbers together. The numbers 1 through 12 (are usually used but you can have as many as you want) are written both horizontally and vertically and all the multiplication facts are written in between. For the problem 9 x 4, you can go over horizontally to the 9 and down vertically to the 4. Where these lines intersect you'll find the answer of 36. You could also go over horizontally to the 4 and down vertically to the 9 and still arrive at the 36 for the answer.

Multiplicative Identity – The multiplicative identity leaves a number unchanged when it is multiplied by one. This is also known as The Identity Property for Multiplication and the Identity Property of one. They state that a number won't change if one is multiplied to the number. The number x one = the same (identical) number. 11 x 1 = 11; 6y x 1 = 6y; ab x 1 = ab

Multiplicative Inverse – The multiplicative inverse always results in an answer equaling one (1). It's taking a number and multiplying it by its opposite, or reciprocal. 5 x 1/5 = 1 (Remember: in fractions, a whole number (numerator) is that number over one (denominator). Taking the reciprocal puts the one on top, as the numerator, and the number on the bottom, as the denominator). 2-1/2 x 2/5 = 1 (The 2-1/2, when converted to an improper fraction, is 5/2).

Multiplier - The multiplier (also known as a factor) is the number that is multiplied "by". 7 x 9 = 63. The 7 is the multiplier.

Multiply – To multiply is to take the multiplier and times it by the multiplicand to equal a product. This is the same as treating the problem as repeated addition (The multiplier (15) is the number that is repeated by the number of times (4) as stated by the multiplicand). 15 x 4 = 60, or 15 + 15 + 15 + 15 = 60; 1/4 x 8 = 2, or 1/4 + 1/4 + 1/4 + 1/4 + 1/4 + 1/4 + 1/4 + 1/4 = 2.

Mutually Exclusive Events – Mutually exclusive events are two events that cannot occur at the same time. This is a statistical term that is used to describe a circumstance where the occurrence of one event is not influenced or triggered by another event, deeming it impossible, or "mutually exclusive," for the events to occur at the same time. When rolling a die once, the outcome is a 1, 2, 3, 4, 5, or 6. You cannot roll a 2 and a 3 on the same roll. Rolling a 2 and a 3 would be mutually exclusive. Choosing a single card in a deck of cards, what is the probability, or what is the chance, of choosing a 7 or a Jack? With one single pick, the card could be a 7 or it could be a Jack, but it cannot be both. This is mutually exclusive event. With the same single pick of one card, what is the chance of choosing a heart or a Jack? With one single pick, the card could be a heart, it could be a Jack, or it could be the Jack of hearts. This event is NOT mutually exclusive.

N – Natural Number through Numerator

Natural Number – A natural number, or whole number, is any number from 1 to infinity (∞). 1, 5, 50, 201, 1,000,000,028 are all natural numbers.

Negative (-) – A negative states that a number is not positive, and has a minus sign in front of it. -6 is a negative number. Positive four (4) and negative two (-2) results in an answer of two (2).

Negative Exponent - The exponent dictates the number of times that the base number is multiplied by itself. Three squared, $3^2 = 3 \times 3 = 9$. A negative exponent equals the number's reciprocal with the exponent then becoming positive. For example, $4^{-2} = (1/4)^2 = 1/4 \times 1/4 = 1/16$, or .0625; $3^{-4} = (1/3)^4 = 1/3 \times 1/3 \times 1/3 \times 1/3 = 1/81$, or .0123…

Negative Integer - Integers include all the negative numbers, all the positive numbers, and zero. Fractions and decimals are not integers. Naturally then, a negative integer is a number less than 0. -45, -12, and -8 are negative integers.

Negative Number (-) – A negative number is a number that is less than 0. -1, -5.25, -3/7, and -5% are all negative numbers.

Neither Composite Nor Prime Number – The only number that is neither composite nor prime is one (1).

Net - Gross is the total of everything. Net is the result of something being removed. Gross pay would include all money earned before taxes and any other deductions that may be taken out. Net pay would include the money left over after all the taxes and deductions are removed from the gross pay. Your gross weight would be the total weight of you, in addition to, your clothes and shoes being on. You net weight would just be the total weight of you, and nothing else.

Net Weight - Gross weight would include the weight of the object along with the box and all of the packaging. The net weight would include the weight of the object only.

Net Worth – The net worth is the total assets minus the total liabilities. An individual has a house valued at $200,000, 2 cars valued at $45,000, other assets totaling $25,000, and cash totaling $3,000. This same person has a mortgage on that house for $125,000, car loans for $30,000, and other loans (credit cards, school loans, etc.) for $25,000. This person's assets total $273,000. The liabilities total $180,000. The net worth ($273,000 - $180,000) is $93,000.

Nominal Number – Nominal numbers are only used for identification purposes. They categorize or name something. They represent nothing of value, quantity, or measurement. The numerical values of nominal numbers are immaterial and unrelated. She wore 8 on her basketball jersey. 98101 is the zip code for Seattle, Washington.

Nonagon - A nonagon (flat-shaped polygon) has 9 straight sides.

Normal Distribution – Normal distribution is a statistical term that shows a symmetrical pattern in the form of a bell-shaped curve for the distribution of a data set. The normal distribution curve is concentrated at the center (the mean, or average) and decreases on either side. Some examples of a normal distribution, but certainly are not limited to, include: people's height or weight, test scores, the amount of sleep people get, the lifespan of a 75 watt light bulb, and many more.

Not Equal ($\neq$) - Not equal is having different values, or to have different amounts of something; not the same. $8 \neq 9$; $5 + 9 \neq 15 - 2$; $5 \times 6 \neq 29$; 3 dimes $\neq$ 1 quarter, 1 dime, and 1 penny

Notation – Notation is a system of figures or symbols used in a particular field to represent quantities, values, numbers, or musical tones. π = 3.1415..., ∞ = infinity

Nought – Nought is an alternative word for zero.

Number – A number describes a value or a quantity, a measurement or a count.

Number Line – A number line (simply a line that is marked with numbers) usually has zero in the center, the negative numbers on the left, and the positive numbers on the right. The number line is useful for displaying number relations, and especially useful for performing the operations of addition and subtraction.

Number Pattern – A number pattern is when a collection of numbers follows a specific pattern or sequence. 1, 2, 3, and 4 follows the pattern of adding one. 3, 9, 27, 81, 243 follows the pattern of tripling.

Number Sense – Number sense is one's ability to comprehend and solve math problems by using numbers and knowing how those numbers work.

Number Sentence – A number sentence is a mathematical problem that is written in numbers and symbols. 5 + 3 = 8; 15 – 6 = 9; 3 x 4 = 12; 63 / 9 = 7. These are all number sentences.

Numeral – A numeral is a symbol (or name) that is used to represent a number. Zero, 0, nothing; 1, one, 3, tri (prefix that means three), three

Numerator – The numerator is the top number in the fraction. It can also be used on the left side, separated by the division symbol, such as 5 / 6. The five (5) is the numerator. The numerator is the part of the whole. If a pizza is cut into 8 slices (this would be the denominator) and I eat 3 of them, I ate 3/8 of the pizza. The 3 (representing slices ate) is the numerator and the 8 (representing the number of slices in the whole pie) is the denominator.

O – Oblique through Oval

Oblique – Something that is oblique (such as lines) is angled, or slanted, in relation to the horizon. It is neither left nor right, nor is it up or down.

Oblique Prism – An oblique prism is a prism whose bases are slanted, or not aligned, with one directly above the other.

Oblong – A rectangle is oblong. To be oblong, the quadrilateral (not a square) has to have four right angles, and two pairs of equal parallel sides, and each pair must be of different length.

Obtuse angle - A geometry term, an obtuse angle is the measure of an angle that is greater than 90 degrees, but less than 180°. If the measure of an angle is less than 90 degrees, the angle is called an acute angle.

Obtuse Triangle – An obtuse triangle has one interior angle that is greater than 90 degrees, but less than 180 degrees (Remember, the three interior angles in a triangle add up to 180 degrees total).

Octagon – An octagon (flat-shaped polygon) has 8 straight sides. A stop sign is in the shape of an octagon.

Octahedron - An octahedron is a polyhedron with eight congruent equilateral triangles. It has eight sides, or faces (Think of an eight-sided die). An octahedron is one of the platonic solids.

Odd Number – An odd number is a number that cannot be divided by two. All odd numbers end with 1, 3, 5, 7, or 9. Examples include: -135, -9, 1, 23, 47, and 2,000,005.

Odometer – An odometer is a device used to measure distance. Usually found on motor vehicles, an odometer measures the total miles, or kilometers, the vehicle traveled.

Ogive – An ogive is a graph (a distribution curve that is a line) of a distribution frequency where the data is cumulative. The ogive helps to locate the median (the middle score) of the data set. Car sales for the year: January, 15 sales; February 12 sales; March 9 sales; April 14 sales. The cumulative frequency would read January, 15 total sales; February 27 total sales; March 36 total sales; April 50 total sales. The ogive would be the line that connects each piece of cumulative data (January through April) to help determine the median of a data set.

Open Curve – An open curve is a curved line that has endpoints, a beginning and an end. The starting and ending points never join.

Open Sentence - A number sentence is a mathematical problem that is written in numbers and symbols. An open sentence contains a value that is unknown, until solved. Depending on the value (or values) used will determine if the solution (open sentence) is either true or false. For the problem $5x - 3 = 17$, $x = 5$ is a false statement (or solution), but $x = 4$ is a true statement.

Operations – There are many mathematical operations that are used to solve problems, or solutions. The four basic operations are the building blocks of arithmetic. These operations are addition (+), subtraction (-), multiplication (x), and division (÷).

Operator – The operator in a problem tells you what to do with the values. For the problem $8 \times 3 = 24$, the "x" is the operator of the problem. It states that multiplying 8 and 3 will result in 24. Using the values 12 and 3, we need an operator to tell us what to do with these numbers because we could get four different answers, depending on the operation. $12 + 3 = 15$; $12 - 3 = 9$; $12 \times 3 = 36$; $12 \div 3 = 4$

Opposite Angles – A pair of vertically opposite angles are formed by the intersection of straight lines and are directly opposite of each other. Each pair of these vertically opposite angles contains the same number of degrees (they are congruent) and the four angles total 360° (degrees). If angle a = 120° and angle b = 60°, then angle c would have to be 120° and angle d would have to be 60°.

Opposite Numbers – Opposite numbers contain the same number but have different signs. 8 and -8 are opposite numbers. The survey has a margin of error of ±3%. Let's say a survey states that 85% of people brush their teeth two or more times a day with a margin of error of +/-3% (+3 and -3 are opposite numbers). This means the actual percentage of people who brush their teeth two or more times a day could range from 82% (-3%) to 88% (+3%).

Order – To order is to arrange, organize, or position something in accordance to its quantity, value, or size.

Order of Operations – The order of operations are rules that state the order in which to solve a mathematical expression. The **P**arentheses come first, followed by and **E**xponents. Then, from left to right, comes **M**ultiplication and **D**ivision, in that order. Lastly, from left to right, comes **A**ddition and **S**ubtraction, in that order. Remember PEMDAS, or the mnemonic device *"Please Excuse My Dear Aunt Sally."* For the problem $(5-2)^2 \times (2-1)^3 + (3^2 \times 2) \times 2 + 16$, we solve it using PEMDAS. **P**arentheses come first $(3)^2 \times (1)^3 + (9 \times 2) \times 2 + 16 = (3)^2 \times (1)^3 + (18) \times 2 + 16$. **E**xponents come next $9 \times 1 + 18 \times 2 + 16$. **M**ultiplication and **D**ivision are next $9 + 36 + 16$. **A**ddition and **S**ubtraction are last. The answer is 61.

Ordered Pair – The ordered pair, or coordinates, are sets of values that point to a specific location on the coordinate plane. For (1, -2), the 1 represents the horizontal x-axis, always the first number, and the -2 represents the vertical y–axis, always the second number. For the ordered pair (4, -1), start at zero on the coordinate plane and go 4 units to the right (x-axis) then 2 units down (y-axis).

Ordering - Ordering is arranging, organizing, or positioning something in accordance to quantity, value, or size.

Ordinal Number – An ordinal number states the place, or position, that something is in. Today is the 29th day of the month. Out of more than 10,000 contestants, you placed 2nd in the National Spelling Bee. The position (29th) and place (2nd) represent ordinal numbers.

Ordinate - This is the distance along the vertical axis, the y-coordinate, on the coordinate plane. The x-coordinate is called the abscissa.

Origin – The origin of something is its starting point. On the coordinate plane, where the x-axis and the y-axis intersect lies the point of origin, or (0, 0).

Ounce (oz.) – An ounce is a unit of measurement that measures weight. 16 ounces equals one pound. One ounce is equal to 28.35 grams.

Outcome – In probability, the outcome applies to the results. Probability states that there is a 16.67% chance of rolling a 7 when throwing 2 dice

Using an online dice roller, rolled 5000 times, the outcome of rolling a 7 was 16.9%. After a second round, the outcome of rolling a 7 was 17.0%. Try it for yourself at http://nces.ed.gov/nceskids/chances/index.asp

Outlier – An outlier is a piece of data that is much further away from the majority of the other values. This data is for example purposes only. These are NOT actual figures. For the past twenty years, the rainfall for the month of March was as follows: 5.3", 5.9", 4.6", 4.8", 6.1", 5.7", 12.9", 6.0", 5.4", 5.8", 1.7", 5.7", 4.9", 5.6", 5.5", 6.2", 5.3", 5.1", 6.0", and 5.2". The outliers for this set of data are 12.9" (much higher than the majority) and 1.7" (much lower than the majority).

Oval – An oval is an egg-shaped, or elliptical-shaped, closed curve.

P – Pair through Pythagorean Theorem

Pair – A pair is two of something in common that usually belongs together.

Palindrome – A palindrome is a number, word, or phrase that can be read both forward and backward. Number palindromes include: 121, 3265623, and 24842. Word palindromes include: racecar, eye, toot, and level. Phrase palindromes include: Do geese see God? A nut for a jar of tuna, and Never odd or even.

Parabola – One of the conic sections, a parabola (looks bowl-shaped) is made by the intersection of a cone by a plane parallel to its side.

Parallel – Being parallel is to endlessly be the same distance apart, all the while never touching.

Parallel Lines – Parallel lines are the same distance apart in the same plane and they never touch (intersect).

Parallelogram – A parallelogram is a quadrilateral (four-sided figure) with parallel opposite sides. The sides are equal in length and the opposite angles are also equal (congruent).

Parameter – A parameter is a value that is already part of, or built into, a function. A function is a mathematical relationship between two values. Every input will result in one output. A function often looks like this: $f(x) = 10 + x$. The 10 is the parameter. A value (input) is put in for x and the result is the output. Depending on the nature of the problem, the parameter(s) can be changed.

Parentheses ( ) – Parentheses are often used to group, or enclose, things together and are the first to be solved using PEMDAS, or the Order of Operations. For the problem $(5 \times 3) + (3 - 2)$, we solve the grouped items in the parentheses first, resulting in $(15) + (1) = 16$.

Pattern – A pattern is a recurring sequence or a design that is repeated. 13151719131517191315 1719…

Pentagon - A pentagon (flat-shaped polygon) has 5 straight sides.

Pentagonal Numbers – The first five pentagonal numbers are 1, 5, 12, 22, and 35. These numbers (the total number of dots needed to take the form of a pentagonal pattern) can be represented in the shape of pentagons.

Pentahedron - A pentahedron is a polyhedron with 5 sides, or faces (Think pyramid – four sides and a base).

Percent (%) – Percent is based on the number 100. If a pizza is cut into 8 slices and you eat 4 slices, you ate 1/2 of the pizza, or 50% of it. Fractions, decimals, and percents are related. 1/10 as a fraction is .10 as a decimal is 10%. He gave all his effort, or 100% of it.

Percentage – Percentage is based on the number 100 (see percent). A very small percentage of people have Doctorate degrees.

Perfect Number – A perfect number is a number (positive integer) that is equal to the sum of its proper divisors, excluding the number itself. Currently, there are 47 known perfect numbers. The first two are 6 and 28. For the perfect number 6, 1 + 2 + 3 = 6. For the perfect number 28, 1 + 2 + 4 + 7 + 14 = 28.

Perfect Square – To square a number is to multiply the number by itself. A perfect square is the number that is made when the whole number is squared. For example, $1^2 = 1$, $2^2 = 4$, $3^2 = 9$, $4^2 = 16$, $5^2 = 25$, $6^2 = 36$, $7^2 = 49$, $8^2 = 64$, $9^2 = 81$, $10^2 = 100$. Therefore, 1, 4, 9, 16, 25, 36, 49, 64, 81, and 100 are perfect squares.

Perimeter – The perimeter is the total distance around the outside of an object, or shape (a circle's perimeter is the circumference). If an equilateral triangle has a length of 8" on one of its sides, the perimeter is 24" (8" + 8" + 8"). If a rectangle has a width of 3' and a length of 4', it has a perimeter of 14' (3' x 2) + (4' x 2).

Perimeter (Square, Rectangle) – The perimeter of a square is 4 times the length of one of the sides. The perimeter of a rectangle is 2 times (length + width)

Permutation – A permutation is an arrangement of objects in a specific order. How many different ways can the letters XYZ be arranged? (6 {3x2x1} – see the multiplication principle) They can be arranged, XYZ, XZY, YXZ, YZX, ZXY, and ZYX

Perpendicular – Something perpendicular is 90° (right angle) to that of the horizon.

Perpendicular Lines - Perpendicular lines are two lines that intersect to form 90° right angles.

Perspective – Perspective is a drawing technique (an illusion depicting volume and spatial relationships, concerning height, width, and depth) that is used regarding the size of objects to simulate distance.

Phi (Φ) – Phi (Greek letter), the "golden number," or golden mean having a ratio of 1:1.618, is better known as the golden rectangle. Phi is an irrational number and has a value of exactly $1 + \sqrt{5}$ divided by 2. The golden rectangle's proportion (1:1.618) is considered "visually pleasing" and has been used since ancient times in art and on buildings.

Pi (π) – Pi, an irrational number, is a ratio of the circumference of a circle in relation to the diameter of the circle. Pi is used to assist in figuring both the area and the circumference of a circle. Some people use the fraction 22/7 to solve for Pi, but 3.14159… is more accurate and more commonly used. For fun, do a web search for "1 million digits of Pi."

Picture Graph – A picture graph uses pictures to symbolize value, or quantity.

Pie Graph (Chart) – A pie graph is a circular chart that gets divided (Think of large pizza pie). Each subdivision (piece) of the pie represents a part of the whole, based on 100%. Each part represents a value, based on some sort of data.

Pint - A pint is a unit of measurement for measuring liquids (volume). One pint equals 1/2 quart, or 16 fluid ounces. 8 pints equals 1 gallon.

Place Value – The place value is the value of a digit, depending on its place within a number. For the number 1,234,567,898,765.4321 the values are as follows: 1 (trillions), 2 (hundred billions) 3 (ten billions) 4 (billions), 5 (hundred millions) 6 (ten millions) 7 (millions), 8 (hundred thousands) 9 (ten thousands) 8 (thousands), 7 (hundreds) 6 (tens) 5 (units, or ones).4 (tenths-1/10) 3 (hundredths-1/100) 2 (thousandths-1/1,000)1 (ten thousandths-1/10,000)

Plan - A plan is a simplified diagram, sketch, or drawing that describes or clarifies something through appearances or structures, explaining how something works or how to assemble it.

Plane – A plane is a flat surface, it contains no thickness, and it extends on forever.

Plane Shapes – Plane shapes are flat, two-dimensional shapes. They can include circles, triangles, quadrilaterals, pentagons, hexagons, heptagons, octagons, nonagons, and decagons.

Platonic Solids – There are five platonic solids. They include the: cube (6 faces), dodecahedron (12 faces), icosahedron (20 faces), octahedron (8 faces), and tetrahedron (4 faces). The faces of the platonic solids are flat and they are made from regular polygons, each of the same size and shape. Think of a die for each of these. A dodecahedron is like a 12-sided die.

Plot – A plot (a physical mark or dot) is a location on a map, or graph.

Plus (+) – The plus sign is the symbol for addition. To plus is to add (sum) two or more numbers together.

PM - It's a Latin word that means post meridiem. It starts at noon, 12:00 P.M., and ends at midnight, 12:00 A.M.

Point (.) – A point represents positioning in space, or an exact location.

Point Symmetry – Point symmetry (Origin Symmetry) is when something (a picture, object, or shape) can be rotated 180° around a point of symmetry (the center) and the image of itself is identically matched (duplicated). This "something" looks the same if it's turned upside down or if it's viewed from opposite directions.

Polar Coordinates – Polar coordinates provide a method of interpreting graphs and indicating the positions (the radius or the polar angle) of points on two-dimensional surfaces (planes).

Polygon – A polygon is a two-dimensional plane shape that must have three or more straight sides; it is a closed plane figure that is formed by line segments. A polygon does not have curves. Polygons include triangles, quadrilaterals, pentagons, hexagons, heptagons, octagons, nonagons, and decagons.

Polyhedron - A polyhedron is a three-dimensional solid shape that is bounded by polygons, which are called faces. The segments where the faces meet are called edges, and the points where the edges meet are called vertices. The five platonic solids are all polyhedrons, as are prisms and pyramids.

Polynomial – A polynomial is an expression (constants, variables, and exponents) that is a monomial or the sum of monomials. Polynomials are combined using addition, subtraction, and multiplication. Division cannot be used when combining polynomials. Also, exponents can ONLY be positive. Some examples include: $2x^3 + y^2 - z + 3$; $2x^2 - y + z^3$; $3x^2y^3 - 4x + 2y^2 - 3$

Population – The population is the whole group of a statistical sample for study. It's the entire set of items (data), or all the individuals (or animals) used as part of the study.

Position – Position is where someone, or something (location), is compared to someone else, or to another object or the surroundings. Three girls came running. The boys weren't too far behind. The dog chased a rabbit (the rabbit is in front and the dog is behind) behind the garden, which is located between the house and the shed.

Positive (+) – Positive is the opposite of negative (-).

Positive Integer - Integers include all the negative numbers, all the positive numbers, and zero. Fractions and decimals are not integers. Obviously then, a positive integer is a number greater than 0. 8, 22, and 125,850 are positive integers.

Positive Number – A positive number is a number that is greater than zero (zero is neither positive nor negative). 8 is positive eight.

Pound - A pound is a unit of measurement that measures weight. 1 pound equals 16 ounces. One ton equals 2,000 pounds.

Power - The power (or power of) commands the number of times that the base number is multiplied by itself. Two to the 4th power is: $2^4 = 2 \times 2 \times 2 \times 2 = 16$; seven cubed, $7^3 = 7 \times 7 \times 7 = 343$. The two and the seven are the bases and the exponents are the ⁴ (pronounced to the 4th power) and the ³ (pronounced cubed). Power is also referred to as the "index," "exponent," or "raised."

Power Set – The power set is all the subsets of a given set. It is written P(S). For the set {1,2,3}, the following subsets can be made: { } = the empty set, {1,2,3}, {1}, {2}, {3}, {1,2}, {1,3}, and {2,3}. The power set, or P(S) = { { }, {1,2,3}, {1}, {2}, {3}, {1,2}, {1,3}, {2,3} }

Prime Factor - A factor is a number that is multiplied together to get another number. A prime factor is a factor that is also a prime number.

Prime Factorization – Prime factorization is a way to write a number as a product of its prime factors. A factor tree is a diagram that can be used to detect prime factors of a composite number. It's writing a number as a product of its prime factors. 36 = "2" x 18; 18 = "2" x 9; 9 = "3" x "3". The number 36 as a product of its prime factors is 2 x 2 x 3 x 3 = 36.

Prime Number – A prime number has only two factors: one and itself. This is a list of all the prime numbers up to 1000 (1 is not a prime number because it only has one factor): 2, 3, 5, 7, 11, 13, 17, 19, 23, 29, 31, 37, 41, 43, 47, 53, 59, 61, 67, 71, 73, 79, 83, 89, 97, 101, 103, 107, 109, 113, 127, 131, 137, 139, 149, 151, 157, 163, 167, 173, 179, 181, 191, 193, 197, 199, 211, 223, 227, 229, 233, 239, 241, 251, 257, 263, 269, 271, 277, 281, 283, 293, 307, 311, 313, 317, 331, 337, 347, 349, 353, 359, 367, 373, 379, 383, 389, 397, 401, 409, 419, 421, 431, 433, 439, 443, 449, 457, 461, 463, 467, 479, 487, 491, 499, 503, 509, 521, 523, 541, 547, 557, 563, 569, 571, 577, 587, 593, 599, 601, 607, 613, 617, 619, 631, 641, 643, 647, 653, 659, 661, 673, 677, 683, 691, 701, 709, 719, 727, 733, 739, 743, 751, 757, 761, 769, 773, 787, 797, 809, 811, 821, 823, 827, 829, 839, 853, 857, 859, 863, 877, 881, 883, 887, 907, 911, 919, 929, 937, 941, 947, 953, 967, 971, 977, 983, 991,997

Principal – The principal is the base (or initial) amount. The principal is invested or borrowed money and includes no interest or dividends. $10,000 is borrowed (principal amount) for a car loan. The interest on that loan is $1,000. The payback amount is $11,000 (principal + interest).

Prism – A prism is a polyhedron (three-dimensional shape) that has flat sides and two identical (congruent) parallel ends (bases) that are shaped like polygons. The prism's name is based on the shape of the prism.

Examples include: triangular prisms, square or rectangular prisms, pentagonal prisms, hexagonal prisms, and octagonal prisms.

Probability – Probability is the chance that a particular event, outcome, or result will occur. Probability is measured as a ratio of the total potential outcomes. The formula is P(event) = number of favorable outcomes / total number of outcomes. Rolling 13 with two dice has a 0% probability. This event has an "impossible" chance of happening. There is a 10% chance of snow tonight. This event has an "unlikely" chance of happening. Calling the correct coin-flip, heads or tails, has a 50-50, or 50% probability. This event has an "even chance" of happening. Labeling 100 Ping-Pong balls 1 through 100 and picking only one has a "likely" chance of drawing a two-digit number (a 90% chance – cannot draw 1-9 single digit, or 100 three digit). A bag contains 10 apples and 10 oranges. There is a 100% chance (probability) you will pull out a piece of fruit. This event has a "certain" chance of happening.

Problem – A problem asks a question in which mathematical operations are used to work out a solution, or answer. A problem can consist of numbers and symbols, words and numbers, or a combination of these.

Problem Solving – To problem solve is to work out a solution, or answer, to solve a problem. To help problem solve, take the words and translate them to mathematics, looking for key words such as: sum and combine (addition), difference between and less (subtraction), times and product of (multiplication), and ratio of and quotient of (division).

Product – The product is the result, or answer, to a multiplication problem. 5 x 2 x 3 = 30; the product is 30.

Proper Factor - A factor is a number that is multiplied together to get another number. 5 x 4 = 20. The 5 and 4 are factors of 20. The complete list of factors for 20 is 1, 2, 4, 5, 10, and 20. A proper factor is all the factors of a number except that number and one. So, the proper factors of 20 are 2, 4, 5, and 10.

Proper Fraction - A proper fraction is when the numerator is smaller, or less than, than the denominator. When simplifying fractions, the final answer always needs to be in "proper" form. Examples of proper fractions are as follows: 1/8, 7/16, 5/9, 3/10, 15/24, 1/100, 3/32, 999/1000. Also, a proper fraction always needs to be reduced to its simplest form. A fraction of 5/10 is a proper fraction. However, its simplest form would be 1/2.

Property – A property is a common feature that something has, such as an attribute, or certain characteristic, a trait, a feature, or a color. An equilateral triangle has three equal sides and three equal angles.

Proportion – A proportion is two or more equal ratios. It can be written as an equation. A 2 to 3 ratio is equivalent to a 6 to 9 ratio. 2:3 = 6:9; or 2/3 = 6/9. The following are all equal proportions: 1/2 = 2/4 = 4/8 = 10/20 = 50/100 = 128/256 = 1,500/3,000.

Protractor – A protractor is an instrument that is used to measure the degrees of angles (0° - 180°). This tool can also be used to draw and create angles.

Pyramid - A pyramid is a polyhedron (three-dimensional shape) that has flat sides and a single base (polygon) that tapers to a point (the top, the vertex, or the apex). The pyramid's name is based on the shape of the pyramid. Examples include: triangular pyramids, square or rectangular pyramids, pentagonal pyramids, hexagonal pyramids, and octagonal pyramids.

Pythagoras – Pythagoras of Samos was a Greek philosopher and mathematician (570 B.C. - 495 B.C) who the Pythagorean Theorem is named after.

Pythagorean Theorem – The Pythagorean Theorem ($a^2 + b^2 = c^2$) is used to solve triangles with right angles (90°). This theorem states that the two sides (the sides that make up the 90° right angle) "a" and "b," when squared, will equal the square of side "c," called the hypotenuse (this is the side directly across from the right angle). Note: the "c" (hypotenuse) is always the longest side. Example: A ramp needs to be built. The height of the ramp will be 5 feet high and will start (on the ground) 30 feet from the building. What is the length of the ramp? We are given the "a" and "b" sides and have to figure out "c." Using the Pythagorean Theorem, $5^2 + 30^2 = c^2$; $25 + 900 = c^2$; $925 = c^2$; we now need to take the square root (the opposite of squaring) of 925. The length of the ramp is approximately 30.4 feet long.

Q – Quadrangle through Quotient

Quadrangle – A quadrangle, another name for a quadrilateral, is a flat-shaped polygon with four angles and four straight sides. A quadrangle can be either convex or concave in shape.

Quadrant (Circle) – A quadrant is one-fourth (1/4th, or 25%) of a circle.

Quadrant (Graph) – Thinking of a coordinate plane, a quadrant is one of four areas (numbered I, II, III, and IV) that is made when the x-axis and the y-axis divides the plane.

Quadratic Equation – A quadratic equation is an equation that contains one or more squared variables, where the highest exponent of the variable is squared. In other words, the exponent can never be higher than a power of two. $2x^2 + x + 2 = 0$; $3x^2 + 4x + 5 = 0$; $x^2 + 3x - 1 = 0$; these are all examples of quadratic equations.

Quadrilateral – A quadrilateral is a flat-shaped polygon that has four sides. Parallelograms, rectangles, rhombuses, squares, trapezoids, and any irregular flat-shaped polygons with only four sides are examples of quadrilaterals.

Quadrillion – One quadrillion is 1,000 trillion. One quadrillion dollars could make one billion millionaires. The number looks like this: 1,000,000,000,000,000.

Qualitative Data – Qualitative data is data that is descriptive, or written with words. No numbers are used.

Quantitative Data - Quantitative data is data that is discrete or continuous, or can be counted or measured. Numbers are always used.

Quantity – The quantity is how much of something (the value, amount or number) there is. I have 100 pennies. The value is $1.00.

Quart (qt.) - The quart is the standard unit to measure liquid, or capacity. Four quarts is equal to 1 gallon. One quart is equal to 4 cups. One quart is equal to 32 fluid ounces.

Quarter – A quarter is 4 equal parts. A quarter is also $0.25, 1/4, or 25%

Quarterly – Something that is done quarterly is done four times per year.

Quartiles – Quartiles, a statistical term, consist of four equal parts (groups or sets of values) into which a population can be divided, based on some variable. Each quartile represents one fourth (25%) of the sampled population.

Quotient – The quotient is the answer to a division problem. 38 ÷ 2 = 19; nineteen is the quotient. In a division problem, the dividend ÷ the divisor = the quotient.

R – Radian through Run

Radian – The radian, which is approximately 57.296°, is an angle that is made via the radius of a circle. It's like literally wrapping the radius around the circumference (outer edge or perimeter) of a circle. The formula is 180/π degrees. If there are 360° in a circle, there are approximately 6.283 radians that make up that circle.

Radical ($\sqrt{}$) – The radical is the square, or cubed root, expression. It's the box that looks like a check mark.

Radicand – The radicand is the number (value) that's inside of the radical box (sign). Taking the square root of 49, $\sqrt{49}$, which results 7, the radicand for this problem is 49.

Radius – The radius of a circle is the distance from its center to the circumference. The radius is 1/2 the distance of the diameter (which is the distance that measures across the whole circle). If the diameter of a circle is 8", then the radius would be 4 inches.

Radius (Polygon) – The radius of a polygon is the distance from the center of a regular polygon to the corner point (the radius goes through the incircle), which is called the vertex.

Radix – The radix is the base of the system of numbers. The base ten, or decimal, number system that uses the digits 0 through 9, has a radix of ten. The binary system (uses 0's and 1's) has a radix of two.

Raise – To raise a number means the same as: "the power of," the "index," and the "exponent." Raising a number instructs the number of times that the base number is multiplied by itself. Three to the 4th power is: $3^4 = 3 \times 3 \times 3 \times 3 = 81$; the three is the base and the "raised" exponent (number) is the ^{4} (pronounced "to the 4th power").

Random – When someone or something is selected at random, the random selection is an occurrence that happens by chance. The choice cannot be predicted. If one-hundred names are placed in a box and one will be selected by random, we know one of the names will be chosen. However, we don't know which name it will be. Rolling a die is random. We know the number will be a 1, 2, 3, 4, 5, or 6, but we don't know which number it will be until the die is rolled.

Random Sample – A random sample is a randomly chosen selection that happens solely by chance. Everything about the random sample is strictly randomized.

Range (Statistics) – Taking the range from a data set is simply taking the difference between the greatest and least numbers, scores, or values in the set of data. For the numbers 10, 8, 15, 25, 31, 6, and 14, the range is 25 (31 - 6). For the heights of students, 5'4", 5'7", 6'0", 5'1", 5'10", and 6'1", the range is 12" (6'1" – 5'1").

Range of a Function – A function is a mathematical relationship between two values. Every input will result in one output. A function often looks like this: f(x). A value (input) is put in for x and the result is the output. The range of a function is the set of all output values of a function. For the function f(x) +3, if the values for x are odd numbers {1, 3, 5 …}, the range, or range of the function, would be {4, 6, 8 …}.

Rate – The rate is a ratio that compares two quantities (numbers or values) that are measured with different kinds of units, or numbers. The car gets a rate of 28 mpg for every gallon of gasoline used. The printer prints 24 pages per minute. The rate is 24 pages can be printed every minute. In ten minutes, 240 pages can be printed.

Ratio – A ratio shows the comparative sizes of two or more amounts, values, or things. If the ratio of a liquid solution is 2 parts concentrate to 5 parts of water, the ratio is a 2 to 5 mix. This ratio could also be written the following ways: 2/5 or 2:5. At a dog show, for every 3 mixed breeds there are 7 purebreds. The ratio is 3:7. This also means that 30% of the dogs are mixed breeds and 70% of the dogs are purebreds.

Rational Expression – A rational expression is the ratio of two polynomials. Because this expression is divided (the numerator is divided by the denominator), defines the expression to be considered "rational." Y^2 + 3 / x - 4

Rational Number - A rational number can be a fraction (3/10), a terminating number (3.185), and it can repeat (3.33333…) or

123.123.123... The following are all examples of rational numbers: 5, -2.3, 2-7/8, -10/5, and 10.287053.

Ray – A ray has no endpoint, but it does have a starting point. Hold a flashlight, point it into the sky, and turn it on. Where you are holding the light is the starting point. From this starting point the light beam will go on forever (assuming that it doesn't bounce off of another object). This is known as a "ray" of light.

Real Number – A real number is any number of normal use, such as any whole (0) or natural number (8), any integer (-75), or any rational (2.5 or 1/8) or irrational (pi or √3) number. A real number is any number that is not an imaginary number.

Reciprocal – Reciprocal is a fancy word that means the opposite (inverse), or in other words, turning the fraction upside down. Taking the reciprocal of the second fraction is the process when dividing fractions. The reciprocal of 2/5 is 5/2. The reciprocal of 2-3/4 is 4/11. The reciprocal of 8 is 1/8. Every number other than "0" has a reciprocal. See also multiplicative inverse.

Rectangle – A rectangle (quadrilateral, parallelogram) is a four-sided polygon with four right angles and two pairs of opposite equal parallel sides.

Rectangular Prism - A rectangular prism is a polyhedron (three-dimensional shape) that has six rectangular faces; two of those faces consist of identical ends (bases).

Recurring Decimal – Recurring decimals have never-ending repeating digits that result in a recurring pattern. 1/9 equals 0.11111...; 1/13 equals 0.076923076923...

Recursive – Something recursive (recurring) comprises of indefinite repeated applications of a rule, formula, definition, or procedure. Example: start with zero, add 5, and then subtract 2. We have 3, 6, 9, 12, 15, 18...

Reduce – To reduce is to simplify (fractions), or to make smaller in number, or in size. For the fraction 8/12, simplifying, or reducing, nets 2/3. Take the number 50 and reduce it by half (50%). The answer is 25.

Reflection – A reflection is a mirrored view of a shape or an image; flipping a figure across a line.

Reflection Symmetry – Reflection symmetry reflects half of a shape, or image, and creates an identical mirrored image. The reflection is divided along the line of symmetry. This is a line that is midway between the object and its mirrored reflection. The original point is on the opposite side of the line. This reflection is flipped and the size does not change.

Reflex Angle – A reflex angle is any angle that falls between 180° and 360°.

Regroup – To regroup, or regrouping, is to reorganize the formation of the group. It is a term used for the operations of addition (when carrying) and subtraction (when borrowing).

Regular Polygon – Regular polygons consist of all sides and all angles being equal (congruent). If all the sides and all the angles are not equal the shape is an irregular polygon.

Regular Polyhedron – Regular polyhedrons consist of all the faces of the polyhedron being made from identical regular polygons.

Relatively Prime Numbers – Relatively prime numbers (relative primes or co-prime numbers) have exactly one common factor, the number one (1). 17 and 20 are relatively prime numbers. The factors of 17 are 1 and 17. The factors of 20 are 1, 2, 4, 5, 10, and 20. The only common factor of 17 and 20 is one. 9 and 10 are relatively prime numbers. The factors of 9 are 1, 3, and 9. The factors of 10 are 1, 2, 5, and 10. The only common factor of 9 and 10 is one.

Remainder – After dividing a number, the remainder is the number, or amount, that is left over. 17 ÷ 3 results in 5 whole, with a remainder of 2 (because another group of 3 could not be made, the 2 is the leftover amount). The remainder as a result of simplifying an improper fraction is placed in the numerator spot of the mined number. 17 ÷ 3 = 5 whole and 2 over 3, or 5-2/3

Repeating Decimal - Repeating decimals have never-ending repeating digits that result in a recurring pattern. 1/7 equals 0.142857142857...; 1/3 equals 0.33333333333...

Revolution – A revolution is going completely around, or one whole spin. A revolution, or full rotation, is one complete turn of 360°, a full circle.

Rhombus - A rhombus is a four-sided parallelogram with parallel opposite sides, which are equal in length, and equal opposite angles.

Rhythmic Counting – Rhythmic counting emphasizes the use an object, or by tapping, to generate a catchy beat to help count in patterns or sequences.

Right Angle – A right angle is equal to 90°. It's one-fourth of a full circle.

Right Triangle – A right triangle is a triangle that has one angle (of the three angles) that measures exactly 90°.

Rigid – Something that is rigid is not flexible and cannot move. It is in a fixed position and cannot be changed. It cannot be bent or forced out of shape.

Rise – The rise is how far a line extends upward or downward (y-axis). The rise is determined by the number of units, up or down, that are counted (The "rise" divided by the "run" equals the "slope" of a line).

Roman Numerals – Roman numerals is a number system that was invented by the ancient Romans that is still used today. One (1) = I, five (5) = V, ten (10) = X, twenty (20) = XX, twenty-five (25) = XXV, fifty (50) = L, one hundred (100) = C, five hundred (500) = D, and one thousand (1000) = M. The year 2012 would be written: MMXII

Root – Taking the root is a mathematical operation indicating which unknown number, multiplied by itself a specific number of times, equals the number included inside the root sign (the box that looks like a check mark - √). The "square root" of 144 equals 12 is an example of a root.

Rotation – During a rotation, there is a point that stays fixed (in the center) and everything else travels around that point in a circular movement. Think of the Earth's rotation. The Earth spins (rotates) on its imaginary axis once every 24 hours.

Rotational Symmetry - Rotational symmetry (turning symmetry) is when something (a picture, object, or shape) can be rotated around a point (the center) and the image looks the same, or it matches its original identity. This "+" has rotational symmetry. Push a pin through the center and turn it 90° to the left or 90° to the right. It can also be rotated 180° either way and this plus symbol will look exactly the same as it did prior to the rotation.

Round (Rounding) – Rounding is the process of changing a number to a more convenient value, all the while keeping its value similar. To round a number, look for the digit that has to be rounded. This digit will either remain the same (if the number is four or lower-called rounding down) or it will increase by one (if the number is five or higher-called rounding up). After the rounding is decided, some of the remaining numbers will become zeros or will fall off. For the number 1,560, rounded to the nearest thousands, the 1 needs to be increased to a 2 (because the next digit is a 5). 1,560, rounded to the nearest thousands, is 2000. For the amount $465.50, rounded to the nearest dollar, the 5 needs to be increased to a 6 (because the next digit is a 5). $465.50, rounded to the nearest dollar, is $466.00, or $466. For the number 654.321, rounded to the nearest hundredths, the 2 remains a 2 (because the next digit is a 1). 654.321, rounded to the nearest hundredths, is 654.32.

Row - A row is an organization of numbers, or values that are one next to the other. The numbers are arranged horizontally. In Microsoft Excel, the rows are 1, 2, 3, 4, etc.

Ruler – A ruler is used to measure distance, usually inches (12 inches) on one side and centimeters (30 centimeters) on the other side. It can also be used to draw straight lines.

Run - The run is how far a line extends left or right (x-axis). The run is determined by the number of units, left or right, that are counted (The "rise" divided by the "run" equals the "slope" of a line).

S – S.I. Units through Symmetry

S.I. Units – S.I. Units, which stands for Système International d'Unitès, or the International System of Units, is the modern form of the metric system that uses seven base units that revolve around the number ten. The seven units are: the meter (m), used for length, the kilogram (kg), used for mass, the second (s), used for time, the ampere (A), used for electrical current, kelvin (K), used for thermodynamic temperature, the candela (cd), used for luminous intensity, and the mole (mol), used for the amount of substance.

Sample – A sample is a small (usually) selection that is taken from the entire population. This selection (sample) examines, or studies, hypotheses made by researchers to help learn about the overall population.

Sample Space – The sample space, often denoted as "S", is the set (list) of all potential outcomes. Drawing one number from a hat that contains the numbers one through ten, S = {1, 2, 3, 4, 5, 6, 7, 8, 9, 10}.

Scale – A scale is a weighing device. It can measure weight, such as grams, ounces, kilograms, or pounds. A scale can be used to measure. On a map, a scale could be 1 inch represents 50 miles. Therefore, two cities that are 4 inches apart on a map are 200 miles apart in reality. Also, to scale in size means to make larger or smaller. A 4" x 6" picture enlarged 100% of its size would increase to 8" x 12".

Scalene Triangle – A scalene triangle is a triangle that has three different interior angles and three sides of different length.

Scatter Plot (Scatter gram, Scatter diagram) – A scatter plot is a graph of plotted points that show a relationship (graphic representation, or correlation) between two variables (dependent and independent), or sets of data.

Scientific Notation – Scientific notation is a unique way of writing very small or very large numbers. The number is written in two parts: a number between 1 and 10 that places a decimal after the first digit, followed by a power of 10. Numbers that are greater than 10 use powers of 10 that are positive. Numbers that are less than 1 use powers of 10 that are negative. For the number 510, the scientific notation form is 5.1×10^2. For the number 16,000, the scientific notation form is 1.6×10^4. For the number 1.0525, the scientific notation form is 1.0525×10^0. For the number .00358, the scientific notation form is 3.58×10^{-3}. For the number .0000025, the scientific notation form is 2.5×10^{-6}.

Score- A score is a numerical value (or a count) that measures something. The score of the basketball game was 84-78, in favor of the visiting team. A score of something equals 20. In Abraham Lincoln's Gettysburg Address, "Four score and seven years ago…" this represented 87 years. Four score (4 x 20) + (7) and seven years ago…

Secant (sec) - The secant of an angle, which is found in a right triangle, is the hypotenuse (the "C" side or the slope) divided by the adjacent side of the hypotenuse. It is equal to 1/cosine.

Secant (Line) – The secant is a line that intersects two or more points on a curve.

Second – A second is a unit of time that is equivalent to $1/60^{th}$ of a minute. There are 3,600 seconds in an hour and 86,400 seconds in a day. One year has 31,557,600 seconds.

Second Hand - The second hand is the fastest of the three hands on an analog clock and represents the seconds of a minute. It takes 1 minute (60 seconds) for the second hand to circle the clock once, and 60 round-trips to equal one hour.

Section – A section is a portion of something bigger. If there is a pizza and a slice is removed from it, a section of the pie has been removed.

Sector – A sector (it looks like a piece of pie), limited by two radiuses and an arc, is a section, or part, of a circle.

Sector Graph – A sector graph is similar to a pie chart. It is a circular chart that gets divided (Think of large pizza pie). Each subdivision (piece) of the pie represents a part of the whole, based on 100%. Each part represents a value, based on some sort of data.

Segment - A segment, limited by a line (chord) and an arc, is a section, or part, of a circle. It's like taking that piece of pie and cutting the crust end off. This crust piece that is left over is the segment of the circle.

Semicircle - A semicircle is one-half (1/2, or 50%) of a circle. It contains an arc (180°) and the diameter.

Septagon - A septagon (flat-shaped polygon) has 7 straight sides. It is also called a heptagon.

Sequence – A sequence (shapes, numbers, or objects) is usually arranged by some sort of rule, or by some special order, or pattern. 3, 6, 12, 24, 48, 96… This sequence starts at three and doubles every number thereafter.

Set { } – A set is a gathering of items and contains "unique" things (numbers, shapes, or objects). Each member is an "element" of the set. {B, C, D, G, J, O, P, Q, R, S, U} is the set of letters in the alphabet that has a curve.

Shape – A shape is a pattern or formed outline of an object. Shapes can be two-dimensional, such a triangles, rectangles, squares, and circles. Shapes can also be three-dimensional, such as cubes, prisms, pyramids, and spheres.

Sharing – Sharing is to split, or divide something into equal portions, or groups.

Short - A short is a block of 1. Math manipulative blocks that show base 10 numbers values. One (1) three-dimensional block is called a "short." Ten (10) three-dimensional blocks stacked on top of one another is called a "long." One hundred (100) three-dimensional blocks stacked ten high and ten wide, 10 x 10, is called a "flat." One thousand (1000) three-dimensional blocks stacked ten high, ten wide, and ten deep (looks like a cube), 10 x 10 x 10, is called a "block."

Side – A side on a two-dimensional shape is called a line, and a side on a three-dimensional object is called a surface.

Side View – The side view it looking at an object from its side.

Sieve of Eratosthenes – The Sieve of Eratosthenes is a way to identify prime numbers that pertain to a set. It was created by the Greek mathematician Eratosthenes of Cyrene (276 B.C. – 195 B.C.). For the set of numbers 1 through 100, start with the first prime number, 2 (1 is neither prime nor composite), and remove all the multiples of two, or all the even numbers. Next, go to the next prime number, 3, and remove all the multiples of three (the ones that are left). Now, go to the next prime number, 5, and remove all the multiples of five (the ones that are left). Lastly, go to the next prime number, 7, and remove all the multiples of seven (the ones that are left). The remaining numbers are prime numbers: {2, 3, 5, 7, 11, 13, 17, 19, 23, 29, 31, 37, 41, 43, 47, 53, 59, 61, 67, 71, 73, 79, 83, 89, 97}. For a larger set of numbers, the pattern would continue by using the next prime number, 11, then 13, then 17… and so on.

Sign – A sign uses symbols instead of words. While driving, seeing a picture of a deer means one is in a deer crossing path. In math, a sign tells the mathematician what to do with the numbers, values, amounts, data, etc. Listed are some of the many symbols (signs) that are used to help solve math problems: addition (+), subtraction (-), multiplication (x), division (÷), decimal point (.), equals (=), greater than (>), pi (π), set ({}), percent (%), dollar sign ($), degree (º), and infinity (∞).

Similar – Something that is similar is basically the same (ex. same shape). A square that is 3" on each side is similar to a square that is 2" on each side. The shape is not the same size, but the outline is the same, they are both squares, or similar to one another.

Simplifying – Simplifying an expression is to solve it. $3(x+2) + 2(x+3) = 37$; $3x+6 + 2x+6 = 37$; $5x+12=37$; $5x = 25$; $x=5$. Simplifying a fraction to its simplest form is to reduce it. $8/24 = 1/3$.

Sine (sin) - The sine of an angle, which is found in a right triangle, is the opposite side (of the hypotenuse, the "C" side or slope) divided by the hypotenuse.

Size – The size of something is how big or small it is. A cat is small compared to a lion. A basketball is larger than a golf ball. A million dollars is a large sum of money compared to a thousand dollars, and a thousand dollars is a large sum of money compared to eight dollars. 0.0001 is minute compared to 10.

Skew Lines – Skew lines, existing in three-dimensions only, cannot intersect or be parallel. Regarding space, skew lines do not lie in the same plane.

Skewed Data – A statistical term, skewed data is data that tends to lie more to one side of the mean (based off of the normal distribution curve). The data (called distorted data) is not symmetrical to the mean (average), or to the "bell curve." For the set of test scores {99, 96, 62, 61, 60, 60, 58} the mean (average) score is 71. The mean test scores is being skewed by the two high scores (called outliers). Sometimes using the mean is not the best way to analyze data.

Skip Counting – Skip counting is counting, either forwards or backwards, by figures other than one. Skip counting by fives: 5, 10, 15, 20, 25...

Slide – To slide something is to move it around in any direction without flipping, or rotating it. Sliding a shape around is called translation.

Slope – The slope of a line is a measure of the incline (how steep it is) of the line. The slope indicates both the direction of the line and the steepness of the line.

Smaller – Something smaller is reduced in size, amount, or in number. Of the numbers 15 and 7, seven is the smaller of the two numbers. A mouse is smaller than a groundhog.

Solids (3D shapes) – A solid is a three-dimensional object (or shape). It has length, width (or breadth), and height. Cones, cubes, cylinders, prisms, pyramids, and spheres are examples of three-dimensional shapes.

Solstice - The summer solstice (June 21-longest day of the year) and the winter solstice (December 21-shortest day of the year) are the two days that the sun it at its greatest distance from the celestial equator.

Solution – The solution is the answer to a problem. For the problem 10 + 10, the solution is 20.

Solve – To solve is to work out the correct answer; to find a solution to a problem. I want to carpet an area in my basement. How much carpet do I need is the dimensions of the room are 20' long and 16' wide? Area = length x width. Area = 20 x 16, or 320 square feet. This problem has been solved.

Sort – To sort is to group, or arrange, in a certain (specific) way. Objects or things can be sorted by color, size, shape, alphabetically, or numerically.

Space – Space is a three-dimensional area (place) in which objects can exist or where events can take place. A Toyota Corolla takes up less space than a dump truck. A mother takes up more space than an infant.

Speed – Speed is a measurement (usually miles/kilometers per hour) that determines how fast something is moving/traveling, or how far it travels over time. The formula to determine speed is: speed = the distance ÷ time. We traveled 400 miles in 7 hours. The average speed was 57.1 miles per hour.

Sphere – A sphere is a solid three-dimensional object, and is perfectly round; like a baseball. All surface points are equal in distance from the center of the object.

Spiral – A spiral is a curve (a path) that goes around some fixed central point. As the curve gets longer, it moves further and further away from the center. A three-dimensional spiral is called a helix.

Spreadsheet – A spreadsheet is a computer program, mainly used for accounting, which manipulates and organizes data. The figures (numbers, amount, values) are arranged in rows and columns on a grid.

Spring Balance – A spring balance is a device used for measuring weight (force). The scale (balance) works once an object is placed on it. The weight is determined by how far the spring moves. Think of the type of scale (spring balance) found in supermarkets to measure produce.

Square - A square (flat-shaped polygon) has 4 straight sides, all of equal length. Every angle in a square is a right angle, 90°.

Square Centimeter (cm^2) – A square centimeter is a unit of measurement (metric) used to measure small areas. It is a square unit (the shape of a square) that measures 1 centimeter on each of its sides. A standard sheet of paper (8-1/2" x 11") is approximately 237.5 square centimeters. (8.5" x 11") x (2.54) = square centimeters. There are 2.54 centimeters in an inch.

Square Foot (sq. ft.) - A square foot is a unit of measurement used to measure semi-large areas, such as rooms or the total area of a house. It is a square unit (the shape of a square) that measures 1 foot on each of its sides. A room that measures 16 feet by 12 feet is approximately 192 square feet. (16' x 12') = square feet.

Square Inch (sq. in.) – A square inch is a unit of measurement used to measure small areas. It is a square unit (the shape of a square) that measures 1 inch on each of its sides. A standard sheet of paper (8-1/2" x 11") is 93.5 square inches. (8.5" x 11") = square inches.

Square Kilometer - (km²) – A square kilometer is a unit of measurement (metric) used to measure large areas. It is a square unit (the shape of a square) that measures 1 kilometer on each of its sides. Think of one kilometer as a very large square that measures 1,000 meters (almost 3,281 feet) on each of its sides.

Square Measure - A square measure is a unit of measurement (metric and imperial systems) used to measure area. It is a square unit (the shape of a square) that measures a unit of length, or distance, (centimeter, inch, foot, yard, meter, kilometer, or mile) on each of its sides. Multiplying the length x width will equal the area, in squared units. An area that measures 25 feet long and 20 feet wide will result in 500 square feet.

Square Meter (m²) - A square meter is a unit of measurement (metric) used to measure semi-large areas, such as rooms or the total area of a house. It is a square unit (the shape of a square) that measures 1 meter on each of its sides. A room that measures 6 meters by 4 meters is approximately 24 square meters. (6' x 4') = square meters.

Square Mile - (sq. mi.) – A square mile is a unit of measurement used to measure large areas. It is a square unit (the shape of a square) that measures 1 mile on each of its sides. Think of one square mile as a very large square that measures 5,280 feet (the number of feet in a mile) on each of its sides.

Square Numbers – A square number is the outcome of multiplying a number by itself. $5^2 = (5 \times 5) = 25$; $12^2 = (12 \times 12) = 144$

Square Root (√) - Taking the square root is a mathematical operation indicating which unknown number, multiplied by itself, equals the number included inside the root sign (the box that looks like a check mark). The "square root" of 81, $\sqrt{81}$, equals 9. The "square root" of 49, $\sqrt{49}$, results 7.

Standard Normal Distribution – A statistical term, the standard normal distribution is the distribution that occurs when a normal random variable (standard score or "z" score) has a mean (central value) of zero and a standard deviation of one.

Standard Notation – A number that is in "standard notation" is the exact same as it is written. The following numbers are in standard notation: 1, 50, and 286

Statistics – Statistics is the branch of mathematics that studies data. It deals with the collection, organization, interpretation, analysis, and presentation of numerical data. Statistics is particularly useful in drawing general conclusions about data (a sample), and generally tries to compare, or connect it to the entire population.

Stem-and-Leaf Plot – A stem-and-leaf plot is a display (plot) of data that shows this data being arranged by place value. Each value is split into a "stem," usually the first digit(s), and a "leaf," usually the last digit. For the following test scores of 65, 70, 72, 73, 75, 81, 83, 87, 90, 95, 98, and 100, a stem-and-leaf plot could read as follows: stem = 6, leaf = 5; stem = 7, leaves = 0, 2, 3, 5; stem = 8, leaves = 1, 3, 7; stem = 9, leaves = 0, 5, 8; stem = 10, leaf = 0. Keep in mind that a stem-and-leaf plot is usually arranged in columns (stem/leaf) and rows (6 – 5; 7 – 0, 2, 3, 5), and so on.

Step Graph – A step graph is a graph that uses "steps" to show data, instead of lines. The graph increases (the same for an interval, then changes for the next interval) in steps, resembling that of a staircase.

Straight Angle – A straight angle is a straight line. It measures 180°. A straight angle is half a circle.

Straight Line - A straight line is a straight angle that does not bend or curve. It measures 180°. A straight line is half a circle. A straight line is the "shortest distance between two points."

Strategy – A strategy is a way to arrive at an answer, or how to reach a solution. It is a plan (blueprint) or a method (technique) that is used.

Subitising – Subitising promptly knows the number (value) or the amount of something without actually counting it. When rolling a die, if a six is rolled it is a known number. One doesn't actually have to count the dots to verify that the number is indeed a six.

Substitution – Substitution replaces the letters with numbers. For the problem, $x^2 + y - 3$, if $x = 2$ and $y = 5$; $2^2 + 5 - 3 = 4 + 5 - 3 = 6$

Subtract – To subtract is to take something from another. If there are 8 pies and 5 are given away, then how many pies are left? 3

Subtract (Minuend) - In a subtraction problem, the minuend is the digit that is subtracted "from." For the problem $12 - 4 = 8$, the minuend is the 12. (Note: the 8 is the difference and the 4 is called the subtrahend)

Subtract (Subtrahend) - In a subtraction problem, the subtrahend is the digit that is subtracted. For the problem $16 - 7 = 9$, the subtrahend is the 7. (Note: the 9 is the difference and the 16 is called the minuend)

Subtraction - Subtraction is taking something from another. If there are 7 puppies in a litter and 6 find homes, then how many puppies are left? 1

Successive – Something successive is consecutive; it follows in an uninterrupted order, or sequence, one after the other. The football team won 15 successive games. 2, 4, 6, 8, 10, and 12 are successive even numbers.

Sum – To sum is to add two or more numbers that result in a total. The sum of 15 and 15 is 30. The sum of 3 dimes, 2 nickels, and 3 pennies results in $0.43.

Summary Statistics – Summary statistics is a numerical summary of information (data) that provides a quick and simple description of data. It can include the mean (average), the median (middle number), the mode (the number that appears most often), the range (the difference between the largest and smallest values), and others.

Supplementary Angles – Supplementary angles are two angles that add up to exactly 180°. Two 90° right angles are supplementary. Two angles that are 28° and 152° respectively are supplementary angles.

Surd – Surd is another name for an irrational number. The $\sqrt{5}$ is surd because it cannot be broken down, or simplified, further. The $\sqrt{9}$ is not surd because it can be broken down further. It can be broken down to 3.

Surface – The surface is the outside layer of an object that can be flat or curved. The surface of an object can be in either two or three dimensions. A cone has both a flat and curved surfaces. Sandpaper has a rough surface and a shiny new car has a smooth surface.

Surface Area – Surface area is the total amount of area (only on the surface) of a three-dimensional shape, or object. Surface area is measured in square units. A cube that is 5 inches (on all six sides) has a surface are of 150 square inches (6 x 5^2).

Surface Area of a Rectangular Prism – Surface Area = (2 x Length x Width) + (2 x Width x Height) + (2 x Length x Height)

Surface Area of a Sphere – Surface Area = 4 x π x r^2

Survey – A survey is a method of collecting data and gathering information. It's usually done by taking a small sample of something (checking the chlorine level in a swimming pool) or by asking people questions such as: Where is your favorite place to vacation? The beach, a Caribbean island, a romantic country, Walt Disney theme parks, or with out-of-state relatives?

Symbol - A symbol replaces the use of words. While driving, seeing a picture of a big "H" means one is in a hospital zone. In math, a sign tells the mathematician what to do with the numbers, values, amounts, data, etc. Listed are some of the many symbols (signs) that are used to help solve math problems: addition (+), subtraction (-), multiplication (x), division (÷), decimal point (.), equals (=), greater than (>), pi (π), set ({}), percent (%), dollar sign ($), degree (°), and infinity (∞).

Symmetry – Object symmetry is (An object is symmetrical) when it reflects half of a shape, or image, and creates an identical mirrored image. The reflection is divided along the line of symmetry. This is a line that is midway between the object and its mirrored reflection. The original point is on the opposite side of the line. This reflection is flipped and the size does not change.

T – Table through Two-dimensional

Table – A table consists of information (words, numbers, values, etc.) that is arranged in columns and rows. A table could be set up that gives a breakdown of yearly utility expenses. The columns (left to right) could be water, sewer, trash, security, television, electric, gas, phone, and internet. The rows (top to bottom) could list the months for the current year. The information would then be recorded in the appropriate column and row. January's electric would be recorded, and so on. At the end of the year, the table would be complete and the year's utility expense table would be neatly organized.

Tables – A multiplication tables table can be arranged to help learn multiplication facts. The columns (left to right) will list the numbers one through twelve. The rows (top to bottom) will also list the numbers one through twelve. The rest of the numbers are filled in (both columns and rows) to complete the chart as follows: 2, 4, 6…; 3, 6, 9…; 4, 8, 12…; and so on. To know what 9 x 7 is, select the 9 (either on the column or row), and 7 (the opposite what you chose before; if you selected the row for the 9, select the column for 7). Now, follow to where the 9 and 7 intersect to arrive at the answer of 63.

Take-Away - To take-away is to subtract, decrease by, minus, or take the difference of. 20 take-away 15 equals 5

Tally – To tally is to use some sort of special mark to count. The score of the soccer game is 18 for the Wildcats and 14 for the Badgers. The tally would look like this: Wildcats |||| |||| |||| ||| Badgers |||| |||| ||||

Tangent (Right triangle) (tan) - The tangent of an angle, which is found in a right triangle, is the opposite side (of the hypotenuse, the "C" side or slope) divided by the adjacent side.

Tangent (Line) – The tangent of a line is where the line precisely touches a curve at a given point. The line does not go through the curve, it only touches it.

Tangram – A tangram is a Chinese puzzle that is simply a square cut into seven pieces. The 7 pieces consist of: 2 large triangles (50% of the area of the square), 1 smaller triangle (about half the size of the two large triangles), 2 even smaller triangles (about half the size of the middle-sized triangle), 1 square (the size of the two smallest triangles put together), and 1 small parallelogram. These pieces can be arranged in different ways to create unique pictures and designs.

Temperature – Temperature is a measure of how hot or cold something is. A thermometer is used to measure temperature, usually measured in degrees Fahrenheit (°F) or degrees Celsius (°C). Celsius is sometimes referred to as Centigrade.

Tenth – One tenth (1/10) is ten equal parts of a whole. A dime is one tenth of a dollar.

Term – A term is any one of the numbers in a series, a sequence, or an expression. For the series …20, 21, 22…, the numbers 20, 21, and 22 are all terms of the series. For the sequence 6, 12, 18, 24…, the numbers 6, 12, 18, and 24 are all terms of the sequence. For the expression 2x + 14 = 20, 2x, 14, and 20 are all terms of the expression.

Terminating Decimal – A terminating decimal ends; its number of digits is a finite number. 1/16 = 0.0625; 1/25 = 0.04; and 10.12345. These are all examples of terminating decimals; they all have an ending point. 1/3 = 0.333…; 1/9 = 0.111… These are examples of non-terminating decimals; they do not have an ending point. These digits will repeat forever.

Tessellation – A tessellation is a pattern that is created with the use of identical shapes (there can be more than one shape used but they must all be identical). These shapes cannot overlap, and they must all fit together without any openings, or gaps.

Tetragon - A tetragon is a four-sided polygon; it's another name for a quadrilateral.

Tetrahedron - A tetrahedron is one of the platonic solids. The faces of platonic solids are flat and they are made from regular polygons, each of the same size and shape. A tetrahedron is a polyhedron with four faces. It looks like a pyramid-shaped die.

Theorem – Mathematic theorems are rules that are expressed through formulas and symbols. A theorem is an idea that uses already known facts to prove a new idea. The most well-known theorem in math is the

Pythagorean Theorem ($a^2 + b^2 = c^2$). Another well-known theorem is the Fundamental Theorem of Arithmetic.

Thermometer - A thermometer is used to measure temperature (how hot or how cold something is), usually measured in degrees Fahrenheit (°F) or degrees Celsius (°C). When taking the boy's temperature, the thermometer read 100.2° (the normal temperature for a human is 98.6°). He had a slight fever.

Third – A third (1/3) is a whole of something broken into three equal parts. Also, he placed third (position) in the race, just behind the two girls, who placed first and second.

Thousand - A thousand (1,000) is a whole number. It is the first four-digit number. 10 x 10 x 10 = 1,000. One thousand (1,000) three-dimensional blocks stacked ten high, ten wide, and ten deep (looks like a cube), 10 x 10 x 10, is called a "block."

Thousandth - A thousandth is 1/1,000 of something. One thousandth is taking something and dividing it into 1,000 equal parts. One millimeter is one one-thousandth of a meter.

Three-Dimensional – A three-dimensional object (having three dimensions) is anything found in the real world; a person, a car, a blade of grass, a pencil, a juicy steak, etc. These objects all have three dimensions: height, width (breadth), and depth (length).

Thrice – Thrice means three times, three times as much (many), or threefold. She was married three times, or thrice married. 33 is thrice 11 (3 x 11 = 33); 11 threefold (11 + 11 + 11) = 33

Time – Time, a continuing order of events, is measured in many ways. To know the time of day, clocks are primarily used. They display the hours, minutes, and seconds. Time can continuously take place over days, weeks, months, years, decades, centuries, millenniums, and beyond. Time can also be measured in segments. The television show will be on from 7:00 PM until 7:30 PM. The race lasted more than three hours. She ran a mile in under four minutes (recorded by a stopwatch). Some people even tell time using a sundial; an instrument that shows the time of day by the shadow of a pointer that is cast by the sun.

Time Line – A time line is a diagram that shows when things have happened over a period of time. These events are positioned on a line, usually referenced by a date or some other unit of time (month, year, decade, and so on). Here is a time line of US Presidents from 1933 to 1981: Roosevelt 1933 to 1945; Truman 1945-1953; Eisenhower 1953-1961; Kennedy 1961-1963; Johnson 1963-1969; Nixon 1969-1974; Ford 1974-1977; and Carter 1977-1981.

Times (x) – Times simply means to multiply. 8 times 7 equals 56 (8 x 7 = 56)

Times Tables – Times tables are basic multiplication facts. A times tables chart can be arranged to help learn these multiplication facts. The columns (left to right) will list the numbers one through twelve. The rows (top to bottom) will also list the numbers one through twelve. The rest of the numbers are filled in (both columns and rows) to complete the chart as follows: 2, 4, 6…; 7, 14, 21…; 11, 22, 33…; and so on. To know what 12 x 5 is, select the 12 (either on the column or row), and 5 (the opposite what you chose before; if you selected the row for the 12, select the column for 5). Now, follow to where the 12 and 5 intersect to arrive at the answer of 60.

Ton – One US ton is equal to 2,000 pounds. African elephants can range in weight from 5,000-14,000 pounds (2.5 to 7 tons).

Tonne (t) – One metric ton is equal to 1,000 kilograms (almost 2,205 pounds).

Top View – The top view is what is seen while looking directly above an object.

Total – Total is the answer to an addition problem. 1 + 2 + 3 + 4 + 5 = 15; the 1, 2, 3, 4, and 5 are called the addends. 15 is called the total.

Transformation – A transformation is a change in position or direction. Although the position or the direction has changed, the object's size and shape has not changed. The basic moves regarding a transformation include a turn (rotation), a flip (reflection), or a slide (translation).

Translation – A translation is moving a shape or object simply by sliding it around into any direction. No flipping or rotating can be involved. Other than being in a different location, the shape or object looks exactly the same prior to the translation.

Transversal – A transversal line is a line that crosses at least two other lines.

Trapezium – A trapezium is a quadrilateral with no parallel sides.

Trapezoid – A trapezoid is a quadrilateral with only one pair of parallel sides.

Trend Line – A trend line illustrates the general direction that a group of points appear to be heading on a graph.

Tree Diagram – A tree diagram is a representation of all the possible outcomes in a sample space.

Tri – Tri is a prefix that means three. A tricycle has three wheels. A triangle has three sides.

Triangle - A triangle (flat-shaped polygon) has 3 straight sides that result from the union of three line segments that are determined by three non-collinear points. There are six different triangles: equilateral (three equal sides and three equal angles), isosceles (two equal sides and two equal angles), scalene (no equal sides and no equal angles), right-angle (consists of one 90° angle), acute (three interior angles all less than 90°), and obtuse (one interior angle than measures greater than 90°).

Triangular Numbers - The first five triangular numbers are 1, 3, 6, 10, and 15. These numbers (the total number of dots needed to take the form of a triangular pattern) can be represented in the shape of triangles.

Triangular Prism - A triangular prism is a polyhedron (three-dimensional shape) that has two identical triangular ends (bases).

Trigonometry – Trigonometry is the branch of mathematics that is associated with the sides and angles of triangles and the calculations, and with the related purposes of any angles.

Trillion - A trillion contains a one, followed by twelve (12) zeros. A trillion ($1,000,000,000,000) dollars can create one million millionaires.

Trinomial - A trinomial is a polynomial that has three terms, 4x + 3y - 2; $2x^2$ + 3y + z^2; $2x^2y$ – 3x + 5

Triple – To triple is to make something three times larger. Our sales total tripled from one month to the next. Fifty cars were sold in March and 150 were sold in April. Tripling 5 is 15; 5 x 3 = 15, or 5 + 5 + 5 = 15.

Turn – To turn is to rotate about a point (center), or axis.

Turning Symmetry - Turning symmetry (rotational symmetry) is when something (a picture, object, or shape) can be rotated around a point (the center) and the image looks the same, or it matches its original identity. This "o" has rotational symmetry. Push a pin through the center and turn it any way you want, the amount of degrees, left or right, as much as you want. Whatever you choose, this symbol will look exactly the same as it did prior to turning (the rotation).

Twelve-Hour Clock – A twelve-hour clock breaks a full day (24 hours) down into two 12 hour time periods. These periods are AM and PM. The beginning of each new day, 12:00 AM, is known as midnight. Halfway through the day, 12:00 PM, is called midday, or noon. 10:30 in the morning is 10:30 AM and 10:30 in the evening (or, at night) is 10:30 PM.

Twenty-Four Hour Clock - A twenty-four-hour clock (better known as military time) uses a full day (24 hours) to state the time of day. AM and PM are not used. The beginning of each new day, 00:00, is known as midnight. Halfway through the day, 12:00, is called midday, or noon. 10:30 in the morning is 10:30, and 10:30 in the evening (or, at night) is 22:30. 07:00 in the morning is sometimes read 0-seven-hundred hours. Seven o'clock in the evening is 19:00, sometimes read nineteen-hundred hours.

Twice – Twice is two times, or two times as many. Roll the dice twice (two times). He rode his bike twice as far as he did yesterday. He rode 15 miles yesterday and 30 miles today.

Two-Dimensional - A two-dimensional object (having two dimensions) has length and width (breadth). Shapes are two-dimensional objects.

U – Undecagon through US Standard Units

Undecagon - An undecagon (flat-shaped polygon) has 11 straight sides. This polygon is also known as a hendecagon.

Unequal (≠) – Unequal is not equal. It does not have the same value, amount, or quantity. $2^2 + 3 ≠ 8$

Uniform Cross-Section – A uniform cross-section (from a solid object) is a cross-section that is identical in shape and size as its base.

Unit – A unit is one of something. It could be one when counting things (a single unit), or it could be a single person, or it could be a single group.

Unit Fraction – A unit fraction is when the numerator (top number) is one. 1/3, 1/4, 1/7, 1/10, and 1/50 are unit fractions.

Unit of Measurement – A unit of measurement is any quantity that can be used as a standard form of measurement. Some area units of measurements are square centimeters, square inches, square feet, square yards, square meters, square kilometers, square miles, and acres. Some capacity (volume) units of measurements are tablespoons, teaspoons, milliliters, ounces, pints, liters, quarts, gallons, and barrels. Some length (distance) units of measurements are centimeters, inches, feet, meters, yards, kilometers, miles, and light years. Some mass (weight) units of measurements are grams, ounces, pounds, kilograms, and tons. Some temperature units of measurements are Celsius, Fahrenheit, and Kelvin. Some time units of measurements are nanoseconds, microseconds, milliseconds, seconds, minutes, hours, days, weeks, months, years, decades, centuries, and millennia. Some power units of measurements are BTU's, calories, foot pounds, horsepower, watts, joules, and kilowatts.

Unit Price – The unit price is the cost of something (per the unit of measurement) you want to buy. Gas is $3.63 (on 2/18/12) per gallon. A pound of cheese is $5.99. Therefore, 1/4 pound of cheese will cost $1.50.

Unit Rate – The unit rate is a comparison (ratio) of two things in which one of them has 1 for a value. Winning on a scratch-off ticket is 1 in 4.2. This means that in every 4.2 tickets bought there will be one winner. The price (unit rate) of pencils is 15 for $1. One pair of sneakers cost $59.99.

Unit Vector – A unit vector is a vector with a length (magnitude) equaling one.

Univariate Data - Univariate data is data that contains one variable. A frequency distribution table is generally used for univariate data analysis. Let's look at text messaging for one week as an example. On Monday, 10 text messages were sent/received. On Tuesday, 15 text messages were sent/received. On Wednesday, 12 text messages were sent/received. On Thursday, 18 text messages were sent/received, and so on. The number of text messages sent/received per day (10, 15, 12, 18…) is an example of univariate data.

Universal Time – Universal Time (Greenwich Time, Greenwich Mean Time (GMT), Zulu time) is the mean solar time for the meridian at Greenwich, England. It is used as a basis for calculating time throughout most of the world.

Unlikely - In mathematical probability, the likelihood of an outcome, or desired result, is measured on a scale, ranging from 0 to 1. If the conclusion is 0, the event, or outcome, is impossible; there is a 0% chance of it happening. If the conclusion is 1, the outcome is said to be "certain" to happen; there is a 100% chance that it will happen. If there is a 25% chance of an event, or occurrence, happening, the outcome is said to be "unlikely," or improbable that the event will happen.

US Standard Units – US Standard Units are those which are used in the United States. Examples include: Area (square inches, square feet, square yards, square miles, and acres), Capacity and Volume (tablespoons, teaspoons, ounces, pints, quarts, gallons, and barrels), Length and Distance (inches, feet, yards, miles, and light years), Mass and Weight (ounces, pounds, and tons), Temperature (Fahrenheit), Time (nanoseconds, microseconds, milliseconds, seconds, minutes, hours, days, weeks, months, years, decades, centuries, and millennia), and Power (BTU's, calories, foot pounds, horsepower, watts, joules, and kilowatts).

V – Value through Vulgar Fraction

Value – The value of something is monetary worth or numerical amount. The value of a dime is $0.10. The value of a quarter is $0.25. A low-end new car may cost around $25,000. The value of 15 + 14 equals 29. Find the value for x: 3x + 6 = 21; 3x = 15; x = 5. The value for x equals five.

Variable – A variable is a symbol (usually a letter) that is used to represent an unknown number. For 7x + 6 = 27, the "x" is the variable (The 7 is the coefficient and the 6 and 27 are constants). For the trinomial x^2 + 2y – 8 both the "x" and the "y' are variables.

Vector – A vector is a quantity that possesses both magnitude and direction. This vector is commonly represented by a directed line segment whose length signifies the magnitude and whose location in space represents the direction.

Venn Diagram – A Venn diagram is a diagram that generally uses circles (sometimes enclosed in a large rectangle) to show relationships among different sets of things. The two circles overlap (intersect). Common elements of both sets will fall into this overlapping area. Circle #1 contains the elements {6, 12, 18, 24, 30, 36, 42, 48, 54, 60}; Circle #2 contains the elements {8, 16, 24, 32, 40, 48, 56, 64, 72, 80}; The intersection (overlapping area) would include the elements {24, 48} since they are multiples of both 6 and 8.

Vertex – The vertex is the common endpoint of two rays that form an angle.

Vertical – Something vertical goes up and down (top to bottom). The y-axis on the coordinate plane is vertical.

Vertically Opposite Angles - A pair of vertically opposite angles are formed by the intersection of straight lines and are directly opposite of each other. Each pair of these vertically opposite angles contains the same number of degrees (they are congruent) and the four angles total 360° (degrees). If angle a = 150° and angle b = 30°, then angle c would have to be 150° and angle d would have to be 30°.

Vertices – Vertices is the plural form of vertex.

View – To view an object (three-dimensional) is to see it in one of three ways: from the "top," from the "front," or from the "side."

Vinculum (—) – The vinculum is the horizontal line that is used to separate the numerator and the denominator in a fraction. It can also be used to indicate that a group of numbers, or symbols, is to be treated as a single group; 1 / (2+3) x (4÷2)

Visual Estimation - Visual estimation is to make a rough approximation (guess) or calculation (through observation and thought), and it is usually concluded by a rounded figure that is close to the right answer. Seeing a full school auditorium with about 25 rows of seats and about 100 seats in a row gives me an estimated guess that there are about 2,500 people in the auditorium.

Visualize – To visualize is to see something inside your head, creating a mental image of an object or a math problem; mental math is a form of visualization.

Volume – Volume is the amount of space that a three-dimensional object occupies; it's the number of cubic units that are required to fill a space. If a cube is 6 inches in length, width, and height, its volume is 216 cubic inches (6 x 6 x 6) = 216.

Volume of a Cone – Volume = 1/3 x π x r^2 x h

Volume of a Cylinder – Volume = π x r^2 x h

Volume of a Rectangular Prism – Volume = length x width x height

Volume of a Sphere – Volume = 4/3 x π x r^3

Vulgar Fraction – A vulgar fraction is a "common" fraction. 1/4, 7/5, and 5/8 are vulgar fractions.

W – Week through World Time Zones

Week – A week is a unit of time that lasts for a period of seven days.

Weight – The weight of an object is determined by gravity (gravitational pull). Someone who weighs 180 pounds on Earth would only weigh 30 pounds on the moon (the gravitational pull on the moon is approximately 1/6 to that on Earth; however, the mass remains the same).

Whole – The whole of something is all of it; everything. The whole job is complete. The whole pizza was eaten within ten minutes.

Whole Number – A whole number is any number (counting number) from zero to forever (infinity). Any negative number, any fraction, or any decimal is not a whole number. 0, 1, 5, 8, 250, 399, and 1,000,000,000,000 (one trillion) are all whole numbers.

Width – The width (breadth) of something is the distance across from side to side. The width of an Olympic size swimming pool is 82 feet (25 meters). The length is 164 feet (50 meters).

World Time Zones – World time zones are based on Universal Time and it begins its measurement at Greenwich, England. Beginning here, one hour of time difference increases (East of Greenwich, England) or decreases (West of Greenwich, England) every 15° longitude (4 minutes for every degree°). For the Eastern Time Zone (New York), the time difference is -5. This means that it is five hours less in New York than in Greenwich, England. If it is 12:00 AM on January 1, in Greenwich, England, it is 7:00 PM, December 31, in New York.

X – X-axis through X-intercept

X-axis – The x-axis is the horizontal line (left to right) of a graph that is found on the coordinate plane. This line assists the x-coordinate's value to help reference that point to a specific location on the coordinate plane.

X-coordinate (intercept) – The x-coordinate (sometimes referred to as the x-intercept) is the position of a point (coordinate) according to the x-axis. Coordinates are sets of values that point to a specific location on the coordinate plane. For (3, -2), the 3 represents the horizontal x-axis, always the first number, and the -2 represents the vertical y–axis, always the second number.

Y – Yard through Y-intercept

Yard – A yard is a unit of measurement that measures length, or distance. A yard is 3 feet in length (36 inches). A football field is 100 yards in length (300 feet).

Y-axis - The y-axis is the vertical line (up and down) of a graph that is found on the coordinate plane. This line assists the y-coordinate's value to help reference that point to a specific location on the coordinate plane.

Y-coordinate (intercept) - The y-coordinate (sometimes referred to as the y-intercept) is the position of a point (coordinate) according to the y-axis. Coordinates are sets of values that point to a specific location on the coordinate plane. For (2, -4), the 2 represents the horizontal x-axis, always the first number, and the -4 represents the vertical y–axis, always the second number.

Year - A year is a unit of time that lasts for a period of 365.25 days. Every 4 years we have "leap year" to make up one additional day (to make up for the ".25" days in a year). There are 365 days on a calendar from January through December. Every four years February adds a 29th day (366 days total for that year) to make up this extra day.

Yield – The yield is the amount of "return" something gives. When farmers harvest their fields, they acquire their yield of crop. Investors earn a yield when their investment earns them money.

Z – Zero through Zero (of a function)

Zero – Zero (0), the whole number between -1 and 1, means to have nothing. I have no money in my pocket. I have $0.00; 12 – 12 = 0

Zero Property of Multiplication – The zero property of multiplication is a rule that states that the product (to multiply) of zero and any number is zero. 15 x 0 = 0; (5 – 5) x 3 = 0

Final Thoughts

I hope that you found this Math Terms and Definitions resource extremely helpful. Thank you for purchasing this educational eBook. Good luck in the future with your mathematical journey, wherever it may lead.

About the Author

Mark Curry earned a Bachelor's Degree in Elementary Education with a mathematics concentration from East Stroudsburg University, located in East Stroudsburg, Pennsylvania. He also earned a Master of Education Degree in Elementary Education, also from East Stroudsburg University. Mark has taught basic mathematics through beginning algebra at a New Jersey state prison for nearly six years. Mark is married to Kristie and they have two daughters; Alexa, who is seven-years-old and Abigail, who went home to the Lord shortly before birth in 2007. They currently have an unborn son on the way.

Printed in Dunstable, United Kingdom